Desktop Publishing

Other books of interest

The Amstrad PC 1512 – A User's Guide
Joseph St. John Bate and Ross Burgess
0 632 01919 0

MS/PC DOS Prompt
Randall McMullan
0 00 383288 0

WordStar Prompt
Randall McMullan
0 632 01914 X

Office Automation Using the IBM Personal Computer Systems
Ross Burgess and Joseph St. John Bate
0 00 383104 3

SuperCalc Prompt
Second Edition
Randall McMullan
0 00 383417 4

Working with dBase II
M. de Pace
0 00 383251 1

*Fourth Generation Languages
under DOS and UNIX*
Joseph St. John Bate
and Dinesh Vadhia
0 632 01833 X

The PICK Operating System
Joseph St. John Bate
0 00 383160 4

Desktop Publishing

**Joseph St John Bate and
Kirty Wilson-Davies**

BSP PROFESSIONAL BOOKS

OXFORD LONDON EDINBURGH

BOSTON PALO ALTO MELBOURNE

First published 1987

British Library
Cataloguing in Publication Data
Bate, Joseph St. John
  Desktop publishing.
  1. Desktop publishing
  I. Title   II. Wilson-Davies, Kirty
  070.5'028'5416   Z249.3

ISBN 0–632–01895–X

BSP Professional Books
Editorial offices:
Osney Mead, Oxford OX2 0EL
  (*Orders*: Tel. 0865 240201)
8 John Street, London WC1N 2ES
23 Ainslie Place, Edinburgh EH3 6AJ
52 Beacon Street, Boston
  Massachusetts 02108, USA
667 Lytton Avenue, Palo Alto
  California 94301, USA
107 Barry Street, Carlton
  Victoria 3053, Australia

Set by V & M Graphics, Aylesbury, Bucks
Printed and bound in Great Britain by
Mackays of Chatham, Kent

Contents

Preface

It is not often that the world of personal computing is shaken by a major new development. In desktop publishing, however, we are witnessing just such a development and the need to keep abreast is paramount if organisations and PC users are to benefit from this new technology.

With the advent of the first commercially acceptable personal computer, many pundits predicted that the 'paperless office' was on the horizon. Nothing could have been further from the truth. For the past 2000 years, society has been shaped by the written word, and experience has now shown that it is not ready for change. Ironically, it is the very same innovation – the PC that was to create the paperless office – that is now a vehicle for the generation of an ever-increasing amount of paper-based communication. Desktop publishing harnesses the power of the personal computer to create paper-based publications that until very recently it required powerful machines and highly skilled craftsmen to produce.

We wrote this book for users and potential users of personal computers who wish to tap into the world of desktop publishing. Our aim is to provide an understanding of the system options available and how they can be most profitably applied.

Profit, control, efficiency and speed of production are the reasons why desktop publishing has attracted so much well deserved attention. Any organisation that uses external typesetting services should, depending on the volume of its published material, be able to show a significant return on investment in a relatively short time – often as little as six months; provided, of course, that it chose the correct system. Moreover, the benefits in terms of raised profile and image, though difficult to quantify, remain important aspects of the desktop publishing process. If an organisation is to be competitive, it can no longer afford to produce unprofessional reports, proposals, or any other documents designed for external distribution.

The book begins with examples of organisations that have used desktop publishing to good effect. The second chapter charts the technical developments and influences that have led to the emergence of desktop publishing. The third chapter outlines the role played by Apple in initiating and developing the desktop publishing revolution and provides an overview of software available on the Apple Macintosh. The application software available under MS-DOS is explained in chapter 4. We also explore the potential limitations to successful desktop publishing in the MS-DOS environment and examine the ways these limitations have been overcome.

For those who wish to develop desktop publishing in the distributed environment, the facilities that are available on multi-user systems are explained in chapter 5.

Chapters 6 and 7 are concerned with add-on peripherals – essential to the desktop publishing process – including laser printers, digitisers, scanners and phototypesetters.

The last chapters of the book are designed to assist the desktop publisher in the production of effective, aesthetic and cost-effective publications – in short, to maximise on the DTP investment. The role of the publisher and the interaction between the participants in the production process is also examined.

While we have selected a cross section of both hardware and software solutions for detailed mention, this is not to imply that many others are not worthy of further investigation. Moreover, given that software is constantly being developed and improved, a definitive overview would prove impossible.

We would like to thank all those friends, colleagues and organisations that have assisted in the preparation of this book. Special thanks to Jo Schurch, who volunteered not only to transfer endless files from the Macintosh to PC-DOS, but proof-read the text as well; to Dinesh Vadhia, who proved invaluable in coping with less simple transfers from Superwriter on the Apricot to WordStar format, and who gave constant moral and technical support; lastly, to Apple Computer (UK) Ltd for the generous use of their Islington Apple Centre facilities.

In the writing of the book we have drawn on our experience as seasoned desktop publishers, not only as dedicated users but also as implementers of desktop publishing systems for authors and corporate organisations alike. We trust you will benefit from all that we have learnt and that this book will smooth your path into the rewarding world of desktop publishing.

Joseph St. John Bate
Kirty Wilson-Davies

Chapter One
Desktop Publishing Means Profit

The excitement and interest in desktop publishing has developed because desktop publishing can be very profitable. The financial return on investment in desktop publishing – hardware, software and training – can be exceptional. Any situation where there is a requirement for printed material should pay for itself within six months. There are systems to suit all pockets and requirements. In this book we will explain what is available, how to use the systems and, more importantly, how to profit from desktop publishing. First let us examine some of the situations where desktop publishing can and does produce profit.

Speed and quality

They demand a complex print job to be done by tomorrow lunchtime. It has got to look first rate and it has got to be done at 40 per cent of the price that would have been charged last year by a traditional printer. Are they slave drivers? Office manager bullies? Corporate dictators? No – they are users of desktop publishing equipment. This is what desktop publishing users are demanding from their systems: speed, quality and bargain basement costs. For the most part, this is what desktop publishing can deliver.

However, desktop publishing is, for many, a totally new concept. If it is totally new to you, do not be concerned. The majority of business people have not heard about the benefits of desktop publishing, but the picture is rapidly changing. People need to know about desktop publishing, the costs of running a system, and how soon a system will pay for itself.

How long does a system take to pay for itself?

From our experience – and we have been involved in numerous projects – desktop publishing systems can pay for themselves within six months: in the course of a single project, according to one accounting professional; two and a half months, quoted an executive in charge of corporate training manuals; six months, said a technical publications manager in a defence contract section at the headquarters of a major multinational company; anything over six months and I wouldn't buy the system, declared the users' evaluator for a major financial institution information division that has installed significant numbers over the period of a year.

Our experiences in desktop publishing took us all over the place, and some of the systems we installed showed a profit after just a few months. Most of these examples date from when the cost of desktop publishing was quite high. Now, with the introduction of the MS-DOS desktop publishing software and the cheap IBM PC clones, the cost of a working system has fallen dramatically. Any individual or company that uses a traditional printer or requires printed documents in volume would certainly profit from the use of a desktop publishing system.

Areas where we have been involved in desktop publishing include the print industry, PR offices, marketing and sales situations, regional newspaper offices, book publishers, traditional company print rooms, political parties, specialist offices, charities, schools and other educational institutions, civil service departments and trade union organisations. All of them, without exception, have profited from the introduction of desktop publishing.

High-tech companies and desktop publishing

An office systems manager of a major high-tech company in Berkshire installed a network of 14 workstations with a total of 300 megabyte hard disk. The publishing network was installed almost three years ago, after a detailed survey of the technology. At the time, they were preparing documents for a Ministry of Defence real time computing system. As soon as the system was installed, a measured productivity increase of 120 per cent was recorded. As the system developed in terms of both hardware and skills training, productivity rose to 650 per cent. The users of the system include a design engineer, technical authors, illustrators and wordprocessor operators.

The case of the Motor Show special issue

A major car manufacturer had a new model announced in time for the industry's largest UK event, the Motor Show. A major opportunity for the editor of the monthly employee newsletter existed, but could it be exploited? The editor wanted to create the maximum interest within the work force on the shop floor by late on Thursday. This was the last chance to reach the night shift before the show opened and began on Saturday.

The big question was how to get the paper out just as the show preparation started to speed into top gear around the company stand. The magazine production schedule straddled the crucial show set-up phases, press review day and the release hour on the embargo press material. The answer was the use of desktop publishing and page layout software linked to a laser printer to produce professional masters. This allowed a local printer to produce the newsletter very quickly using high-speed printers. If the desktop publishing system had not been installed, the newsletter would not have been printed in time.

The increase in productivity among the shop floor workers after they received the up-to-date newsletter could well have paid for the system. The system used was an Apple Macintosh and an Apple LaserWriter printer.

The literary account

At a firm of UK accountants, the professional practice department used Apple computers for audit purposes. They are now also used for desktop publishing activities centred around the LaserWriter in the department. The system includes an Apple Macintosh Plus, and the original LaserWriter which was expanded to three as soon as the system started to pay for itself after a few months.

The firm became involved in in-house desktop publishing when trying to produce a 60 page book. They had 40 pages or more prepared in hard copy, but it took over a month to get the material back from the typesetter, and then it was in galley form. After looking at the final 20 pages, which had a high graphics content, they realised that it was going to take a long time to get it all done. A decision was taken to buy a LaserWriter and page layout software. As a result of this decision, it took a week to finalise the last 20 pages ready for printing. Taking into account the notional time, costs of proofing, and the time going back and forth to the typesetter, the system paid for itself on this project alone.

As well as publishing 60 page specialist booklets, they also produce many of the business forms that are used by the accountants in their everyday activities. The text for publication, produced using Word or MacWrite, is then fed into PageMaker, a desktop publishing software package, where camera ready copy is prepared. It has been reported, on the basis of proposal work produced on the desktop publishing system, that numerous clients have commented positively on the quality of presentation. Clients are also impressed by the speed at which revised galleys can be turned out on site using the ImageWriter.

The case of the ten-pin bowling championship

Two and a half months was the time taken for a desktop publishing system to pay for itself, said the training manager of a major high street photographic dealer. The system is equipped with an Apple Macintosh, 20 megabyte hard disk and a LaserWriter. Although there were no firm figures to go on, the training manager estimated that this kit could certainly pay for itself in six months; in fact, it took just two and a half.

In common with many organisations, the firm used to send out a lot of work to typesetters. An examination of the invoices showed that the cost was around £15 per A4 page of copy set, £65–100 for full blown form with line artwork and half-tones, with a minimum £10 set-up charge. The outlay of £10,000 was covered in just two and a half months. Although most of the initial work was associated with the production of training material, the system is now used for all sorts of jobs. The most unusual job to date was to produce tickets for an interdepartmental ten pin bowling championship.

Dial in a service

Satellite Service in Aberdeen has stolen a march on the printing industry by offering typesetting and full-blown plate setting by Monotype's Lasercomp Imagesetter, one of the most advanced pieces of typesetting equipment on the market today. A recent Satellite customer is a small family book-publishing business in Glasgow that, thanks to the bureau service, now does its own setting at home on the PC. One book project, early in 1986, was in danger of driving the publisher to distraction due to problems in getting clean material from a typesetter. Composition and setting for the 180 page book took two months and cost £2000. Using Satellite Service in late October, the task was completed in less than three weeks.

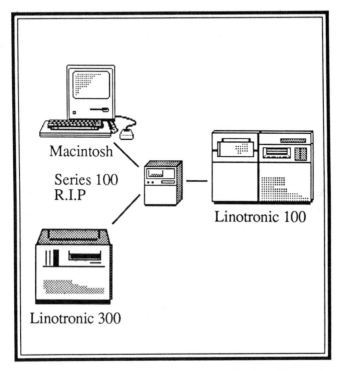

Fig. 1.1   Sample output from Linotype series 100 DTP system.

Even in that time, it was obvious that the system was going to pay for itself. Had the book been done entirely through Satellite Service, the actual cost to the business would have been £500. For any realistic cost benefit comparison, there is also a need to take into account the publisher's time; but even allowing two to three weeks of input time, they are ahead of the game. They also, with this system, achieve exactly what they intended.

According to this company, the three great things you get are control, creativity, and low cost. These and other benefits of desktop publishing are explained in later chapters.

Graphics for Fleet Street

When David Huston, Deputy Features Editor of *The Independent*, learned how to use the Apple Macintosh, he was impressed most by the time-saving that would be possible. He urged colleagues to evaluate the Macintosh and LaserWriter, and *The Independent* now has several as a complement to its Front-End Direct Editorial Input System.

This newspaper has a higher proportion of graphic material than any other on Fleet Street. The cost of an art department for the level of input required would have been much higher than the cost of the desktop publishing system. Pie charts can be completed in 10 minutes instead of having to be ordered a day in advance. The system is so versatile that it has even been used to produce the crossword puzzle!

Profit-making by default

Around the time of moving to *The Independent*, Huston was looking for a way to serve his new readership that had sprung up from the writing community. After experiments with the Apple Macintosh, he knew it might be possible to start a newsletter. His wife also became involved. They bought a Macintosh of their own, and the magazine *Wordsmith* was launched.

Although the project did not aim to make a profit, the use of the Macintosh and desktop publishing software meant that a profit was achieved. The Hustons were also impressed by the standard of output, which they think might have made the publication more popular than had at first been expected.

The case for desktop publishing

Cost justification taxes even the best accountant. There are always as many methods of figuring an assumption to base them on as there are experts in the building, and that is usually too many. Like fitness regimes for athletes, there are reasons why accounting methods vary from company to company. Therefore every company does need to do its own sums. The most tangible type of savings may be in time, but in most companies we spoke to the greatest benefits are in the control over results that desktop publishing gives and the overall quality of those finished results.

There are many benefits to be gained from the application of desktop publishing, and in fact we have yet to find a single company or individual who has bought a desktop publishing system and isn't happy – if not delighted – with the purchase. There are few, if any, applications in the microcomputer market that can boast such satisfaction.

Chapter Two
Technical Developments and Desktop Publishing

The major forces responsible for the 'desktop publishing revolution' have, almost without exception, come from within the microcomputer industry. The professional print and publishing end of the spectrum has only latterly become involved. It is the personal computing industry that forms the vanguard in this particular revolution.

The developments that led from hot-metal typesetters to the fourth-generation phototypesetters of today have not produced desktop publishing. There are similarities, in that the latter two both employ laser technology to build up characters (raster images); but the position is rather the convergence of technologies than some kind of historical linear progression.

Early micros and the publishing process

Publishers and personal computer users in each distinct industry tended to be concerned with their own disciplines. There was no apparent need for cross pollination; the needs, the tasks and the hardware performing those tasks were worlds apart. Or so they thought.

However, in the late seventies the two did meet, if only briefly. Linotype developed the APL series of front ends to run their typesetting software. The APL terminals, available with single or dual floppy drives, are menu driven and hence simple (by the standards of typical typographic processes) to use. APLs provide their own communications software to allow data to be transferred directly, even to remote typesetters, via modem and telephone lines. The APL terminal is a modified Apple II, and the more recent portable APL50 is built around Apple's own portable, the IIc.

Since then, the picture has changed somewhat. Today it is possible to drive a high-quality typesetting machine, such as a Linotype Linotron 100 or 300, directly from an unmodified Macintosh. Indeed, the Linotron acts as another device on Apple's local area network. The only additional piece of equipment required is a raster image processor (RIP) which sits between the AppleTalk network and the typesetter (see Fig. 1.1).

What is significant, at this stage, is an examination of the technological developments that have led to the desktop publishing revolution.

Typesetting and what it means to whom

The terms 'typeset' and 'typesetting' have been bandied about with a lot of other jargon, to such an extent that they mean different things to different people and next to nothing to most of the rest. To clarify the situation, it is necessary to revert to basics. Ultimately, all printed text is typeset since typesetting, by definition, is the setting or organising of letters (type) upon a page. Therefore, by producing documents on a manual typewriter one is effectively producing a typeset page, albeit at the most basic level. Today, however, typesetting is synonymous with the professional system of producing page layout prior to printing, irrespective of the method used.

'Desktop publishing' is in many respects a misnomer, since it is not generally used for publishing but is mainly the system used to compose pages. In short, it is a means of producing screen-based, camera-ready copy, and/or camera-ready artwork without recourse to the cut-and-paste method. The traditional cut-and-paste method involved cutting out bits of text and graphics from various sources and then pasting the results into an acceptable format. The method is time-consuming and requires the application of a high level of skill. Desktop publishing does away with the majority of this activity.

The three key elements

There are three main elements in desktop publishing that can be broadly summarised as follows:

(1) The personal computer, or front end, through which text and/or graphics are entered or into which text and/or graphics are transferred from other sources. This includes the importing of files from other micros, minis and mainframes, and the accepting of images via scanners and digitisers.

(2) The complete desktop publishing system will support output to a

variety of devices including a laser printer with a minimum resolution of 300 dpi, using a Xeroxgraphic technique to output directly on to plain paper. The output device, typically a laser printer supporting a standard page description language, should allow the printing of combined text and graphics. It is desirable that any desktop publishing system be capable of sending the completed camera-ready page/document directly to a professional phototypesetter, producing an output of 1200 + dpi on to light-sensitive paper.

(3) Page layout or typesetting software allowing screen-based cut-and-paste from a variety of software sources and lending full support to the page description language resident in the output device.

In certain cases, particularly in the MS-DOS environment, there may be another component in the form of a user interface, i.e. GEM or Windows. This allows a Macintosh-like emulation effectively to disguise MS-DOS from the user. It also enables the user to carry out complex tasks by selecting an option from a pull-down menu accessed from an icon-based screen (see Fig. 2.1)

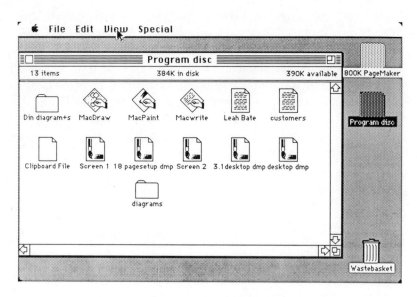

Fig. 2.1 Macintosh icon-based screen.

The constituent parts of the typical single-user desktop publishing system are shown in Fig. 2.2.

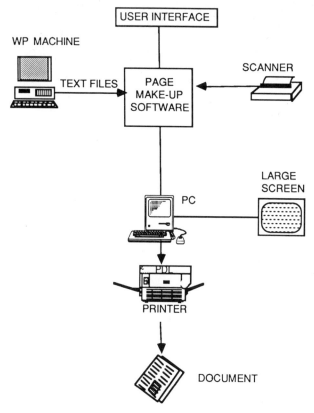

Fig. 2.2 Constituent parts of a single-user desktop publishing system.

The origins of desktop publishing

It is generally accepted that the paperless office many pundits predicted would come about in the late 1980s is a myth. Indeed, recent statistics show that the amount of paper used in offices and homes has doubled over the past seven years and shows every sign of doubling again over the next seven.

The reasons are many, not least being the fact that human nature is slow to change. As a society, we have been using paper for the past 2000 years and are in no hurry to change. There is an inherent trust in information in the form of 'hard copy'. Paper is also very portable.

The effect of wordprocessing

The advent of the microcomputer and the concept of wordprocessing served to enhance the written word. If something becomes more effective, it will be used more frequently. Wordprocessing is very effective, and, as a result, the wordprocessed mailshot and the 'personalised' letter are now widely used; proposals have doubled in length – in short, the amount of paper in circulation has increased.

Graphics add to the picture

As the power of the personal computer developed, and with it new dimensions of graphics software, the production of charts and graphs came down from its traditional place on the dedicated CAD/CAM workstation and the mini/mainframe environment, on to users' desks. Programs such as Lotus 1-2-3 allowed users to create effective business graphics in a matter of seconds. The power of the image as a means of communicating numerical information, statistics, trends, results and forecasts was realised and developed on the personal computer. This has led to the use of even more paper.

The restrictions of printing technology

As the number of wordprocessing and business graphics users increased, the demand for high-quality output escalated. The options were restrictive. One could use a standard dot matrix printer that would allow graphics to be printed but offered very low resolution. The daisywheel printer evolved as the industry standard for text processing, but by its very nature could not print graphics. The NLQ (near letter-quality) dot matrix printer emerged, offering a 24 pin head as opposed to the standard 9 pin version of the traditional dot matrix printer. In simple terms, output resolution was increased and graphics could be printed, but each character was visibly made up of dots and hence not acceptable for anything other than drafting.

Ink jet and thermal printers met with limited success. Ink jet printers were using new and unperfected technology (though they may have a part to play in the future); thermal printers required special paper, and output always appeared rather insipid. To aggravate the situation, there was no software that allowed for the integration of text and graphics. The latter would often be produced on a plotter and appended to text documents.

Laser technology leads the way

It was a technological advance in the form of the low-cost laser printer that did most to forward the cause of desktop publishing. Using a mechanism not unlike that of a photocopier, the laser printer also included a raster image processor (RIP). This was the key to the effective integration of text and graphics. The RIP treats both text and graphics as images to be built up line by line in memory and then re-created on the page. Depending on the available memory resident in the printer, the ratio of graphics to text supported on any one page can vary.

Significance of the page description language (PDL)

The availability of the laser printer alone would not have been sufficient to allow such versatility of output as the desktop publishing function required. It was the implementation of the page description language (PDL), specifically PostScript, that was instrumental in the successful output of combined text and graphics and the use of industry standard fonts.

Windows, icons, mouse, pull-down menus (WIMPs)

The acceptance of the WIMPs environment also helped in the development of desktop publishing. When producing 'what you see is what you get' (WYSIWYG) screen layouts, it is simpler to move blocks of text or graphics with a pointing device such as a mouse than by using keyboard controls.

Furthermore, as a legacy from the CAD/CAM environment, packages emerged that allowed the user to draw on screen, a task that is too cumbersome without the aid of a mouse.

Lastly, the art of page composition is not easy. In the traditional printing environment it is carried out by skilled craftsmen who have undergone many years of training. For the desktop publisher, the simple user interface provided by the WIMPs environment assists in getting to grips with a complex procedure. It reduces most options to the level of icons or pull-down menus and serves to create a very simple method of achieving a sophisticated end.

Software producers cash in

With affordable laser technology in place, an ultra-easy user interface and the ability to integrate text and graphics, it was just a matter of time before software writers took advantage of the available features. In chapter 3 we trace the growth cycle of Macintosh software – the epitome of the WIMPs/WYSIWYG environment – to its current level of maturity. While Apple is universally acclaimed for having taken the lead, many others have followed. The current 'state of the art' in desktop publishing encompasses large numbers of other manufacturers' operating systems and approaches.

The traditional print and publishing industry has influenced events. As mentioned above, the impetus behind the entire desktop publishing revolution stemmed in the main from the PC arena. One cannot overestimate the part played by Xerox in the field of research and development. The fact remains, however, that it was left to a microcomputer manufacturer to make that research a commercial reality.

The publishing industry on the sidelines

The professional publishing industry initially stood on the sidelines, no doubt waiting for the whole thing to blow over. But it didn't. Instead, it grew from strength to strength precisely because desktop publishing software developers looked to the traditional industry for their standards.

As PC-based page make-up software matured, it did so at the expense of the professional typesetter. Not only did desktop publishing adopt the professional jargon (often incorrectly), but increasingly it is adopting the sophisticated standards, such as finely tuned kerning, industry standard fonts, and hyphenation and justification.

The restriction of 300 dpi resolution has hindered the desktop publishing process considerably. It was only when a few innovative typesetter manufacturers, such as Linotype, changed from a passive to an active role that the technologies converged – with overwhelming success.

Fear concentrates the mind

Fear can be the greatest innovator. It was preferable, or so Linotype contended, to work with rather than against an industry that could, given the right technological innovations, edge the established companies out of the business.

So rapidly is the entire industry moving, that desktop publishing has moved on to the notion of electronic publishing. Many desktop publishing systems cannot now be accommodated on a desk, and the provision to link to professional typesetting equipment detracts from the notion of the desk-based solution. It seems that we shall soon be referring to the collective notion of all aspects of computer-based document production as 'electronic publishing'. At the end of the day, however, it is the performance and the results that need to be addressed: the jargon can take care of itself.

Renaissance of embedded codes

Once the initial excitement over the ease of using a WIMPs environment had died down, many desktop publishers started to demand more precision, greater facility for long document runs and sophisticated boilerplate, or style sheet, facilities. Moreover, they were not afraid of sacrificing ease of use to achieve greater flexibility. The same

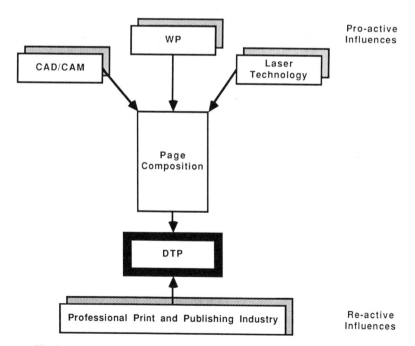

Fig. 2.3 The emergence of desktop publishing – the influences.

is true of almost any discipline. One begins the learning process with the simple approach but moves on to more complex material as interest and the desire for more knowledge increases.

Having provided this basic outline of the developments that led to the emergence of viable desktop publishing (see Fig. 2.3), we can now examine the concept of desktop publishing in terms of the general and specific benefits that may be gained by various user types. In simple terms, the advantages of desktop publishing are fourfold:

- Cost benefits
- Time savings
- Control
- Image/Profile

Desktop publishing can save money

Cost savings can apply to the company/organisation with an annual expenditure on external typesetting services in excess of one-third of the system outlay (since capital expenditure is generally written off over a three-year period). Cost may also be saved in the area of forms production, graphics/artwork design for logos, presentation material and diagrams. As the system becomes familiar to the operators, more and more uses are discovered, devised and implemented.

Time savings

We are all familiar with the production cycle from galley to finished page. We are equally familiar with the time it can take. The beauty of a desktop publishing system lies in the fact that documents can be produced in a matter of hours – not days, as is the case when traditional publishing systems are used.

One situation where the time factor was crucial (and the image of the company was enhanced as a result of time saved) was in the prompt amendment of price lists. A distributor in an extremely competitive market place received notification of substantial price changes from a certain manufacturer. Rather than sending out appendices or addenda to an existing price list, the distributor was able to update the entire document, print a limited run on the laser printer, and ensure that a current price list was on the desks of all major customers the next day. It is in cases like this that a desktop publishing system can pay for itself very quickly.

The same principle applies to the newsletter. In a fast-moving industry such as the computer industry, product information is out of date almost as soon as it is received. Copy must be created, input, laid out and printed within a very short time. Prior to desktop publishing, this meant having a dedicated typesetting and print department on site or making do with wordprocessed and photocopied production.

Control

The constant movement of galleys, paste-ups, proofs and completed documents between originator, typesetter and printer leaves room for human error. However, probably the most frequent cause of hold-up in an already protracted process is the mind-changing syndrome. The ability not only to edit but to allow for author alterations on one system ensures complete control over content and aesthetics. It also ensures that confidential information is protected.

Image/profile

The credibility of companies involved in selling, marketing, PR, and any aspect of media or communications is frequently assessed on the level of presentation. Who would award an advertising budget to a company producing low quality documentation? Only recently, one of the authors received a letter from a 'profile-raising' consultancy specialising in so-called information technology houses. Having scraped away layers of Tippex, the message eventually emerged. The response took the form of a beautifully tailored proposal for the supply of a desktop publishing system!

One must never lose sight of the fact that, while meetings can influence the recommenders and middle management, final buying decisions are generally made at board room level. The only real advantage one may have over competitors, other factors being equal, is the quality of the proposal document. Professionalism in written communication implies professionalism in everything else.

The significance of industry standards

Any publication that deals with microcomputing, however application-specific its content, must address the concept of industry standards, the reason being that the microcomputer industry – indeed, the whole computer industry – has been showered by such a variety of 'standards' as to result in no meaningful standards at all. The situation has been almost unbelievable, and very tiresome.

Imagine the printing and publishing industry working without standards. The paper size might be specified not as A3 or A5 but in terms of inches, millimetres or manufacturer's descriptive labels – such as 'handkerchief', 'pillowcase', 'half-pillowcase', and so on. The sizes might even change for each manufacturer as and when he chose. Ridiculous, certainly, but the micro user has come to expect just such a situation. For the printing and publishing industry it would be unacceptable, but only because that industry has learned to expect a definite continuity and uniformity in commodity specification.

It is essential, therefore, to understand how machine, peripheral and software compatibility is arrived at through the emergence and subsequent implementation of industry standards. Moreover, the prospective desktop publisher should be wary of systems that do not allow for coexistence with other items of equipment, or that lead up blind alleys where upgrading is concerned. In the event that all machines were totally incompatible, each software package would have to be rewritten for each model of computer. This, in turn, would inhibit the development of a mass market and would prevent, for sound commercial reasons, the emergence of a plethora of quality software.

The MS-DOS standard

With the notable exception of Apple, it is now accepted that the only way to ensure a product's success is to follow the MS-DOS standard (although this might change once the new IBM OS/2 has been developed). However, at present, not only do manufacturers have to adopt the MS-DOS standard but they now have to be sure that the disks are standard, the BIOS is standard, the keyboard is standard – in fact, that every machine is a clone of every other. This is now the reality, but for how long?

It is the duty of all consumers to demand a standard. These standards, it should be noted, are not necessarily the best solutions technically. They just mean that the user does not have to worry about learning a different method for each machine.

Standard fonts

There is a preference, although this depends on the kind of user, for industry standard as opposed to 'bastardised' fonts. In the main, true Merganthaler fonts (as devised by Otto Merganthaler, inventor of the first hot-metal composing machines in 1844) should be available. In the event that they are not, one cannot guarantee that the WYSIWYG convention will apply when text is output through a professional typesetting device; hence subtleties such as very precise kerning may be lost or rendered useless in this situation.

Desktop publishing must allow the user absolute control over selection of fonts, font attributes (italics, emboldening, underlining, etc.) and font sizes. Nor should there be any constraints as to the percentage of graphics to text or vice versa in any one page. The system should support at least one serif font – usually Times – and one sans-serif font – typically, Helvetica. Most publications can get by with two typeface families; indeed, the more fonts one tries to use in any one document, the less pleasing will be the result.

A constant 'selling point' of many of the systems offering non-industry standard as opposed to true fonts is the fact that the user has, say, 64 typefaces available to him. The novice desktop publisher throws up his hands in glee, and rejects the eminently more suitable system because of its apparent shortage of fonts!

Input devices

It is desirable, though not essential, for a desktop publishing system to allow for the input of images through various means: scanners, video digitisers and optical character readers. Obviously, problems will arise if images are scanned in at 300 dpi and subsequently output through professional typesetting equipment at a considerably higher resolution. If, however, the scanned image can be transferred to software that supports a page description language, the problem will be overcome. In addition, editing at pixel level, followed by image reduction, would assist in overcoming resolution discrepancies. The standard for any scanning device should be that it produce files in TIFF (Tag ImageFile Format).

Page description languages

The development of desktop publishing has been largely influenced by the adoption of page description languages (PDL) as a mechanism for controlling output. Without the use of a PDL, images would be transferred to the paper pixel by pixel and line by line, a slow process and highly consumptive of memory. The absence of a PDL implies, indeed creates, output device dependency. Software with, for example, PostScript drivers can output not only to the Apple LaserWriter but to all PostScript devices.

PDLs have been classified as the latest type of fourth-generation language (4GL). They can be learned within a few days, and enable users to embed their own PostScript commands in the document to achieve special effects, or specific output commands to improve the efficiency of the desktop publishing system. The presence, however, of a PDL creates the need for significant processing power resident in the printer/typesetting device – Apple's LaserWriter offers more RAM than the Macintosh itself.

PDLs allow output device independence since the output operation is essentially twofold:

(a) Generation by the application program of PDL code for the required page, followed by
(b) Translation of the code by the PDL interpreter resident in the output device to build up an image as defined by the instructions received from the front end.

From New York harbour to desktop publishing

PostScript was the brainchild of Evans and Sutherland, ex-employees of the Xerox Corporation. The original idea of a page description language was conceived while they were employed in research at Palo Alto. Frustrated by the Corporation's lack of commitment to the ongoing commercial development of the project, they left Xerox to go it alone.

They were subsequently commissioned to carry out a harbour simulation project. The concept was to build a digital model of New York harbour to enable the simulator to project the view of the harbour as seen from the bridge of a ship. Finding no suitable means of outputting data of this type, they perfected the original concept of a page description language and came up with PostScript. Evans and Sutherland went on to form Adobe Systems, the vendors of PostScript and a company that has played a key role in the development of desktop publishing.

PostScript as industry standard

There are a number of reasons why PostScript has become the most widely used PDL. First of all, the language required for printing must have a straightforward syntax. PostScript is, like FORTH, a high-level language, because the syntax is so simple to parse. This means that if the user needs to communicate with another processor the serial data can simply be sent across the wire and consumed by the processor on the other side in a straightforward way.

Another advantage is that new computer programs can be generated very easily. The straightforward syntax has made this language a natural choice for a printing protocol because it is procedural based as opposed to being a static data structure.

At the last count, PostScript was supported by 49 DOS-based software products, with another 23 due for imminent release; 36 mini/mainframe packages, with an additional 19 just around the corner; and the majority of Macintosh software packages, too numerous to mention.

Other PDL contenders

Hewlett Packard's recent decision to implement ImageGen's document description language (DDL) has led to an upsurge in its popularity. Also in the running is Xerox's InterPress, which has recently been endorsed and accepted by ICL. Both parties are counting on this collaboration as a means of establishing InterPress as the de facto industry standard – they have considerable catching up to do!

Despite this, Xerox's popular MS-DOS-based document layout package Ventura currently supports PostScript, and will shortly provide DDL drivers. One wonders why Xerox has not implemented its own InterPress, if confidence in the language is so strong.

Other PDLs currently under discussion include Prescribe and Express, both of which purport to allow programming by the illiterate with the use of English-like commands. This does not, however, necessarily imply acceptance. In the field of database software, dBase has remained market leader over a considerable time period despite its marked unfriendliness. There is no reason to assume that late entrants in the PDL race will succeed merely because they purport to be easy.

Chapter Three
Macintosh and Desktop Publishing

The term 'desktop publishing' is said to be the brainchild of Aldus Corporation, Apple Computer, or both. Given that the two companies have worked closely together, let us for the sake of fairness assume the latter and allow the kudos to be shared. If it were not for the Macintosh's eminent suitability for the task, desktop publishing as we know it might not have become a reality, and the publishing revolution currently in progress might never have occurred. One cannot overstate the significant contribution Apple has made in bringing publishing systems within reach of the personal computer user.

Pre-Macintosh developments

Apple took a considerable commercial risk in launching a series of computers that broke away so dramatically from traditional PC conventions. The Apple II, despite its hard-core following, was technically out of date, and the Apple III a fiasco and an embarrassment. Apple was desperately in need of a successful product if it was to retain credibility as one of the leading personal computer manufacturers.

The notion of 'what you see is what you get' or WYSIWYG was alien to the typical PC user. Under traditional CP/M and MS-DOS operating systems, the user would access files and directories through a series of learnt key strokes. The Macintosh, through its innovative use of WIMPs (windows, icons, mouse, pull-down menus) and WYSIWYG, changed all that.

Lisa adopts enhanced SmallTalk

It did not happen overnight. The Lisa introduced by Apple in 1983 adopted and enhanced SmallTalk, the revolutionary language developed at Xerox's Palo Alto Research Center (PARC). SmallTalk was the first object-orientated language that allowed the application developer to produce software utilising the concept of icons (i.e. meaningful pictorial representations of microcomputer nomenclature – files, folders, deletions, copying methods, etc.).

The idea is simple: rather than the operator having to type commands, or select an option from a menu, the screen shows a number of little pictures or 'icons'. The cursor is pointed at the one in question using a non-keyboard input device such as a mouse, and the mouse is clicked. Other features of this type of presentation include 'pop-up' or 'pull-down' menus that appear only when requested. Often the screen is divided up into a number of windows. Some systems have the windows side by side, while others have them partly overlapping, like papers lying around on a desk; each window represents a program or task in progress, or a document being processed. The mouse allows the user to move around easily from one window to another. Figure 3.1 shows a typical Macintosh menu.

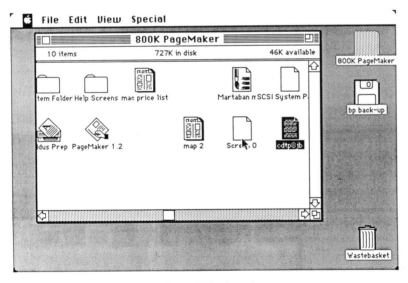

Fig. 3.1   Typical Macintosh menu.

The Lisa had limited success due to three main factors. It was priced unrealistically for the performance levels offered; Apple's idea of a suite of software to cover general office and business application was too inflexible; and the world of traditional micro users was wary of and unprepared to accept, such radical changes.

Macintosh makes an entrance

A second generation machine was called for, one that not only appealed to the user's purse but offered increased flexibility and was aimed at the 'individual' rather than the corporate user. So the Macintosh was conceived, in its original form – an innovative, small, one-box solution (closed architecture, no add-on boards, no options) offering a rather humble 128K of RAM and 400K disk drives.

Initially, the Macintosh fared no better than its predecessor. There is a myth in the computer industry (indeed, it is prevalent in most technical industries) that power is synonymous with complexity. Hence, any computer that permitted users to be up and running in a matter of minutes rather than hours was viewed with suspicion and relegated to the status of toy/designer workstation: trendy and friendly, but not particularly serious.

The need for user-friendly systems

As hardware and software become more powerful, they can also become more difficult to use. As an example of this, take the telephone. Everyone knows how to use the telephone to make a call or to answer a call because the procedures are almost self-evident. There is no switch to turn it on, other than the action of picking up the receiver, which you need to do anyway. The process of dialling is simple because the numbers on the dial correspond to the numbers you have in front of you or in your mind when you make a call.

Nowadays, however, telephones are becoming more sophisticated, and that is where the trouble starts. Modern automatic systems have all sorts of useful facilities: you can dial the last number again without keying in all the digits; you can get the system to keep ringing an engaged extension until it is free; you can tell the system that you are moving temporarily to another extension, and your calls will follow you there.

There is only one thing wrong with having all these facilities: it is very difficult to remember how to use them. Some instruments have a few extra keys with rather obscure letters and codes marked on them, but for the more sophisticated systems the facilities have to be obtained by keying in a numeric code. For full-time telephonists, this is a very good arrangement; but for the executive, who needs a particular facility only once a week or so, the codes become impossible to remember.

The same is true with personal computers. It is all very well to use a PC with Lotus 1-2-3 or an accounting package if you use that package every day. The trouble starts if there are three or four other packages to be used, say, once or twice a month. Unless the system is as self-evident in its use as the telephone, it will not be used at all. More office automation systems fail because of their complexity than for any other reason.

Uniformity of operating procedures

On closer inspection, there appeared to be great advantages in the enhanced icon-based 'finder' adopted as the Macintosh operating system. Not only did it allow true WYSIWYG screen representations, but every software package – third-party and Apple's own – operated in precisely the same way. The user was therefore spared the chore of relearning basic operations every time a new software package was used.

Increased power

RAM upgrades soon became available, as did a new model, the 512K or 'Fat Mac'. At this point, had Apple positioned the product more realistically as a powerful business PC and a viable alternative to the IBM, acceptance would no doubt have arrived sooner.

It was the introduction of the Macintosh Plus, with 1 megabyte RAM and available hard disk options, coupled with the advent of desktop publishing, that caused the computer world not only to sit up and take notice but to put in considerable time, money and research. The Macintosh SE and Macintosh II – new additions to the Apple range – will, while allowing limited compatibility with the MS-DOS environment, continue to uphold their well established standards. Ease of use, epitomised by the WIMPs approach, remains central to Apple's philosophy.

A low-cost publishing system is born

The WYSIWYG environment adopted and advocated by Apple was the perfect vehicle for desktop publishing. Simplicity of operation, coupled with low cost and effective results, offered wide appeal for the creation of camera-ready copy (CRC) and camera-ready artwork (CRA). The benefits were tremendous, not only in terms of time and cost savings but, perhaps most critically, in terms of control. It suddenly became realistic to create, design, amend (again and again, if required) and output entirely on a low-cost desktop system.

However, the advent of true WYSIWYG and a screen adequate to support complex combinations of text and graphics was not enough without an output device able to improve screen resolution. Certainly, the production of a low-cost laser engine, around which Apple could build its powerful LaserWriter printer, was yet another factor contributing to the product's success.

Macintosh leads the way

By adopting certain desktop publishing conventions, the Macintosh total desktop publishing system became the de facto leader, almost by default since little else was available. Industry standards emerged, and it is against these standards that every other desktop publishing system is measured.

Built around the Motorola 68000 32 bit chip, the Macintosh SE, Apple's current top-of-the-range model, is supplied with a built-in 9 inch high resolution screen displaying at 72 dpi, 800K floppy drives, or one 800K floppy and one 20 megabyte Winchester, and 1 megabyte RAM as standard. The current version of the operating system can support up to 4K RAM, and allows a user-definable RAM cache of up to 768K. The following interfaces are supplied: serial, for modems, printers, plotters etc.; SCSI (small computer systems interface), a recently adopted industry standard that provides a fast data inter-change rate and is ideally suited for the attachment of hard disks. An AppleTalk (Apple's low-cost peripheral sharing network) port is also provided. A slot at the back provides the facility for plug-in cards, to be supplied by third-party vendors. It is anticipated that an MS-DOS card will shortly be available, allowing the SE, if used in conjunction with the Apple 5.25 inch disk drive, to run DOS applications.

Hard disk options

With the availability of the SCSI interface, the addition of a hard disk makes the Macintosh a very fast and powerful PC. Various hard disk options are available: Apple's own 20 megabyte HD20 SC which sits neatly underneath the Macintosh, thereby retaining the compact 9 inch × 9 inch footprint, or a wide variety supplied by other manufacturers – Symbiotic, Quisk, MacBottom and Hyperdrive, to mention but a few. The Hyperdrive was the first internal hard disk available for the Macintosh. Initially the installation procedures involved were daunting, though this is now said to have improved.

There is a certain appeal in such a logical development of the one-box solution, and other manufacturers were quick to jump on the internal drive bandwagon. There is now a wealth of such products, offering both SCSI capability for the MacPlus and SE and standard interface for 512K users.

Optimising the Macintosh

Several hardware considerations should be borne in mind by the prospective desktop publisher. While the pros and cons of floppy-disk vs. hard-disk-based systems is covered in greater depth later in the book, the following guidelines are worth noting:

(1) Any serious desktop publishing system should most certainly be based around the Macintosh Plus or the new Macintosh SE. The importance of the RAM, supplied as 1 megabyte upgradable to 4, cannot be overemphasised, particularly in the area of image processing. Use of the SCSI port as supplied with both models speeds up disk accessing quite noticeably compared to previous models.

(2) Consider carefully the purchase of your hard disk. There is a certain wisdom in buying the constituent parts of a system from one manufacturer. Not only does this policy ensure onward compatibility in terms of hardware and software upgrades, but it also assists in the smooth running of maintenance contracts in the event of system failure (which, thankfully, seems to happen less frequently on the Macintosh than on the standard open architecture PC). In addition, dare we mention the aesthetic aspects of such a strategy? The computer is going to be part of the desk furniture for a long time, so it might as well be pleasing to the eye. Beauty and functionality can mix.

The majority of third-party Macintosh hard disks available in the UK are supplied by companies holding distribution rights rather than representatives of the manufacturer per se. Hence, though they may appear better value initially, there might be dangers. Technical support and spares availability might be less than perfect. Symbiotic, a British company, are a notable exception, and their products offer the UK user a viable alternative to Apple's own.

(3) Make use of the available utilities to speed up the Mac's operation. 'Switcher' and 'mini finder' enable you to move from one application program to another without having to return to the desktop (WIMPs equivalent of disk directory) to reload programs.

(4) Do think twice about using an Apple ImageWriter as a low cost proofing device. The Macintosh screen-based fonts were designed with a 72 dpi screen and dot matrix output in mind. The fonts are adequate approximations of their industry standard counterparts. Hence Apple's Geneva is the screen-based equivalent of Helvetica; New York corresponds to Times. Any font referred to by a city name (Monaco, Venice, London, etc.) is an ImageWriter font. A page designed, made up and sent down to an ImageWriter will not, therefore, be an identical representation of the same page produced on the LaserWriter. The ImageWriter has a role, but this should be restricted to the printing and proofing of galleys prior to make-up, and not the finished article.

The Macintosh environment and desktop publishing

The term WYSIWYG, though a relative newcomer to the PC world, originates in the print industry where make-up terminals such as the Xenotron and systems such as Xyvision are already in use. Text can be manipulated with great flexibility, and in some cases half-tones and line drawings can be shown correctly placed on the page.

The Macintosh operating system was geared towards data manipulation and flexibility, making it admirably suited to the desktop publishing task – at a fraction of the cost of its professional counterparts. Moreover, the Macintosh is supplied as a complete unit with the correct hardware and software configuration to allow this to happen. This advantage will become clearer when we go on to discuss the IBM PC and look at the range of add-ons needed to bring that system up to a workable specification.

Most significant, however, is the fact that 'The Apple Macintosh is currently the only desktop publishing system where data interchange between applications is fundamental to the way the computer works' (*Systems International*, Febuary 1987). In effect, the cut-and-paste facility is available as standard, regardless of which application package is in use.

The Macintosh system provides the user with a 'clipboard' – a temporary storage area in which data is held pending pasting into another file/page/document. The 'scrapbook' is a permanent storage area, designed to hold reusable text and images, obtained from any source, for subsequent pasting into the required document.

It was no accident that US software developers Aldus originally selected the Macintosh as the vehicle for their PageMaker package. The rest is history ...

Macintosh software

Before examining in depth the page make-up systems currently available, let us first consider the software elements and the roles they play in total page production. The constituent parts can be broken down under the following headings:

- Wordprocessing software
- Structured graphics
- Freehand graphics
- Business graphics
- Communications
- Page layout

Wordprocessing

Wordprocessing continues to play a major role in the creation of text. The text need not originate on the Macintosh: communications and the ability to pull in files from other sources for subsequent layout are discussed briefly below.

Wordprocessing alone is satisfactory for the production of letters, textual reports or indeed any document that requires neither columns, integrated text, nor sophisticated typographical facilities. If 300 dpi output resolution can be obtained in an industry standard font, it is feasible to refer to the wordprocessing of documents as desktop publishing.

MacWrite

MacWrite, Apple's own proprietary wp software, is more than adequate for standard text production. Though lacking the bells and whistles of sophisticated wp systems, the assumption here is that major text manipulation will be performed in the page make-up package.

Predictably MacWrite offers all the advantages of WYSIWYG operation. Fonts, styles and sizes can be changed throughout the document at will, merely by pointing at and clicking on the portion of text to be changed, or by a rapid scroll through the entire file. Style changes for individual words, headers, etc, can be performed using a toggle principle, i.e. two keystrokes turn the style on or off. Nothing superfluous or meaningless appears on screen, just text in the specified style.

A significant number of functions can be accessed without using the mouse – a boon for the touch typist, who is naturally less than delighted at the prospect of periodically diving for the mouse when keyboard controls would prove faster. Apple have helpfully supplied keyboard equivalents for many of the mouse controls, such as cut-and-paste, align, justify, find, and style changes. Moreover, the controls used are simple to remember because they are totally logical; thus 'B' represents bold, 'U' underline, 'O' outline, 'S' shadow and 'I' italic.

Since text editing is somewhat cumbersome in a typical page make-up system, it is advisable to make all alterations, as far as possible, at the wordprocessing stage.

Figure 3.2 shows a typical MacWrite screen.

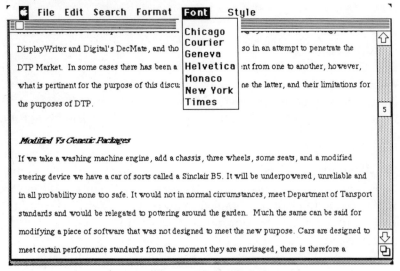

Fig. 3.2 Typical MacWrite screen.

Microsoft Word

Word offers a greater level of sophistication than MacWrite in terms of traditional wp facilities. Indeed, it has been found adequate by some users for the production of books and technical manuals – and this without using a page layout package.

Structured graphics

The creation of organisation and flow charts, technical diagrams, forms, etc. can be subsumed under the heading structured graphics. The uncontested leader among graphics packages of this type is Apple's MacDraw. Able to support the 300 dpi of the LaserWriter, MacDraw offers some interesting features. In addition to what one would expect – lines of varying thickness, boxes, circles, arcs, polygons, a choice of hatches or fill patterns including various shades of grey – MacDraw allows for acceptable precision. On-screen rulers allow specific object sizing, and a grid covering the entire work area allows objects to be easily lined up, using the 'snap to grid' facility that recurs throughout any examination of Macintosh software. Coordinates can be shown on screen to verify that circles and squares are true.

Objects, once created, can be duplicated and aligned against various criteria. A complex image made up of many objects can be 'grouped' in such a way that the constituent parts act as a whole. Grouping allows the easy manipulation of images, through 'dragging' (i.e. grabbing the graphic with the mouse and hauling it around the screen), cut-and-paste or duplication.

MacDraw allows the user to work at actual size or at display-entire-page size. Text can be input directly; up to 48 point size is supported, as are the LaserWriter fonts. Text and objects can be created and placed on top of or behind other objects, creating a collage effect with as many layers as required. Objects can be sent to the back, or brought to the front, according to the result desired. Rotation in any direction, other than through diagonals, is supported.

Lastly, though the LaserWriter limits output to A4-sized chunks, very large documents can be created under MacDraw – a suprisingly powerful package for under a £100. Figure 3.3 shows a typical MacDraw document.

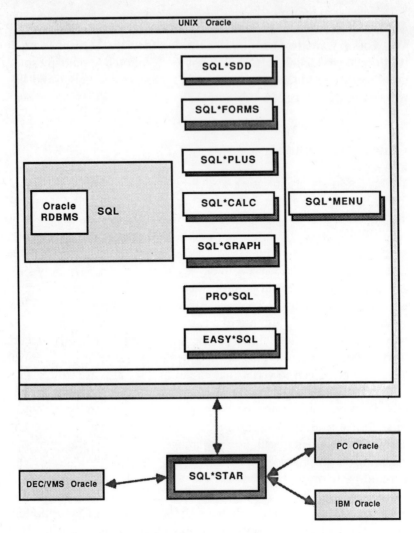

Fig. 3.3 Typical document produced using MacDraw.

Freehand graphics

Freehand graphics allow the production of line drawings that are not dependent on certain specific shapes. Typical applications include the freehand design of logos, cartoons, and illustrations in general. So popular has computer-aided 'art' become that exhibitions are now being held dedicated to this discipline. The most impressive results are best achieved with the use of a graphics tablet and stylus, tools to which the user can more readily relate than to the mouse.

MacPaint is the original freehand drawing package, upon which all others have been based. Available tools, represented in true WIMPs form as icons, include a pencil for fine line drawing, a paintbrush, an aerosol can for the graffiti effect or merely to assist in shading, a paint pot to fill predefined shapes with shades or patterns, the usual squares, lines and circles and, for obvious reasons an eraser. Perhaps Mac-Paint's most useful facility is the 'fat bits' option which allows a portion of the screen to be blown up to pixel level for precise editing. This is an important facility in the editing and general tidying up of previously scanned images. See fig. 3.4, showing a typical example of 'fat bits'.

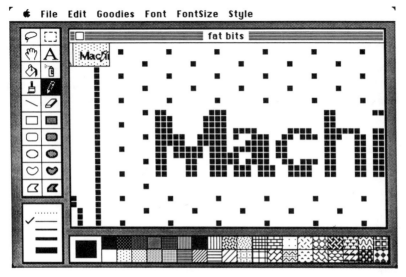

Fig. 3.4   Example of 'fat bits'.

Unfortunately, MacPaint was designed to support the ImageWriter printer and will only output at 72 dpi. Other software houses have been quick to jump on the bandwagon and produce MacPaint clones with full LaserWriter support. The desktop publisher with a need for freehand design would therefore be well advised to opt for FullPaint or SuperPaint. These are third-party packages that have been designed to provide output at 300 dpi.

Business graphics

It is widely accepted that graphs convey trends, results – indeed, any commercial message – more effectively than do columns of fiqures. The manual creation of graphs, however, is tedious and time-consuming, especially if the results keep fluctuating. Business graphics are widely used in the production of financial and statistical reports, presentation materials, published accounts, and any publication that needs to illustrate numerical data.

Business graphics packages cover a spectrum of the most widely used chart and graph styles: scatter, line, bar, column, pie, xy, etc. Traditionally, business graphics were offered as a function of the spreadsheet or integrated software package, the trend having been set by Lotus 1-2-3 in 1984. The beauty of this approach was the ease with which graphs could be replotted when the data changed.

Lotus Jazz

Lotus Jazz was the first serious integrated software package for the Macintosh. The spreadsheet principle allows text and figures to be placed in cells arranged in a grid of rows and columns. Formulae entered perform mathematical and statistical calulations on whatever data relate to that specific cell. In order to produce a graph using Jazz, one merely selects an area of data using the mouse, opens a graphics file, selects the graph type and gives the plot command – all this performed using pull-down menus. The graph appears almost immediately.

At this stage, considerable editing options are available; legends and titles can be arranged using the standard LaserWriter font families; shading and fill patterns can be specified, and of course the graph can be cut or copied into the scrapbook or saved for subsequent use in a page layout program. Any changes to the original data will be reflected in the graph until such time as it is removed.

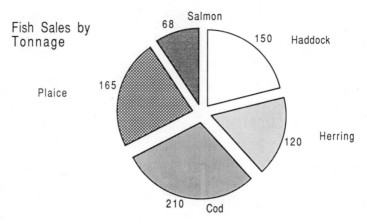

Fig. 3.5 Typical Jazz business graph.

Microsoft Excel

Microsoft's Excel operates in much the same way, but offers enhanced spreadsheeting capabilities. If the idea of using an entire spreadsheet system merely to produce some graphs sounds rather daunting, then opt for a package which performs the latter without the cost of the former. Professional Business Graphics, Cricket Graph serves such a purpose. Figure 3.5 shows a sample graph produced under Jazz.

Communications

Communications software exists to enable text generated on another computer to be imported into the Macintosh for subsequent manipulation and formatting. There is no need, therefore, to relegate existing wp machines to the scrap heap, since text created on the majority of popular systems can readily be transferred, in ASCII format, on to the Macintosh. Why upset the applecart by asking wp operators to learn new systems, when in reality there is no need? This chapter was input on an IBM PC using WordStar and transferred on to the Macintosh using a serial cable and 'MacLink' software. Although some formatting was required at the Macintosh end, the entire operation took about 10 minutes.

So having obtained the prerequisites for text and graphics production, one is ready to proceed to page layout – the essence of the desktop publishing system.

Page layout software

For the sake of clarity, we have outlined the functions of each package before providing a brief overview of relative strengths and weaknesses, as judged against the 'ideal' proposed in chapter 2. We have added some additional criteria, based in the main on personal experience.

Given the wealth of available desktop publishing software, it is impossible to cover every package. The criteria for inclusion were twofold: did the software come close to the ideal, and did we feel it had sufficient following/credibility still to be around in the foreseeable future? As software continues to be developed, some products come to the fore and, as market leaders, enjoy a successful life cycle. Others make an appearance and then, for a variety of reasons, disappear.

Aldus PageMaker – page-based

PageMaker is the most widely used PC-based page composition package available (over 30,000 copies were sold in the first year). Indeed, so significant has its impact been that it can be said to have defined, if not created, the desktop publishing market. It has set standards and become regarded as the benchmark that other software developers must follow if they are to win a slice of the market.

At the time of PageMaker's initial release there was very little around in the way of strong competition: Ready Set Go version 1 was available, MacPublisher in a rudimentary form, and very little else. Hence despite a glaring lack of typographical functions and little concern for aesthetics, PageMaker's simplicity, speed and effectiveness, its ability to manipulate text and graphics from other software sources, and its PostScript support made it a clear winner.

Pre-PageMaker, there were no desktop publishing standards, and no significant products by way of comparison. Futhermore, there was no clear definition, not only of whom the primary users would be, but of what levels of professionalism they would demand. It is only very recently that awareness has increased, and the divide between professional publishers, typesetters and graphic designers on the one hand, and PC users on the other, has closed. The latter are now demanding typographic sophistication previously unknown (and certainly not understood) by the traditional microcomputer user and dealer alike.

The PageMaker functions described below relate to version 2.0, released in February 1987.

Text manipulation

The interactive page composition program provides a screen-based electronic cut-and-paste facility for the production of camera-ready artwork/copy.

Text taken from a wordprocessing package (MacWrite, Microsoft Word) is flowed (snaked) into pre-defined columns. Text can be edited at any stage, through one of the five viewing sizes. ie. entire page, two facing pages, 200 per cent, actual size and 70 per cent. It is not advisable, however, to use PageMaker for text entry. Slow screen redisplay realistically limits the user to minor edits. Any changes made will 'ripple' through the entire document. If text is rearranged to allow space for a graphic to be inserted, the resulting extra text will automatically flow into subsequent columns.

THE DIFFERENCE BETWEEN ENHANCED WP and DESKTOP PUBLISHING

As manufacturers and software developers, desperate to jump on the DTP bandwagon, (in case the so called revolution is qwelled overnight) rush out their product offerings; the tendancy is to take the shortest route to the desired end. It is expedient, or so they think, to beef up a wordprocessing package, add a facility for column support, and provide some links with graphics software. The 'piece de resistance" arrives, of course when they develop a page preview facility, and immediately lay claim to the WYSIWYG environment - the panacea for all DTP software. Despite the Heath Robinson approach, success is quaranteed. Or is it?

The demarcation between true page composition systems and enhanced Wordprocessors is currently quite clear to those who have used DTP in anger. Yet, as it means just about anything to anyone, this confuses the issue somewhat. We have attempted above to define DTP as we understand it, and it is based on this understanding that we examine below enhanced wordprocessing, and its limitations to the desktop publisher. We also examine the potential convergence of the two technologies and the resulting implications.

Wordprocessing

The concept of wordprocessing is simple, it is also, a practise so common that we tend to adopt a blase attitude to the benefits of this remarkable innovation, and wonder how we ever lived without it !

In essence WP is the manipulation and arrangement of words. Unlike using a typewriter, the words do not go directly onto paper: they appear on a screen which becomes the medium for alterations and edits. Only when the entire document is correct is it commited to paper. In this way a great deal of effort is saved, and the operator is free to work at the full typing speed, since any errors can be put right later. The total saving in time can be quite dramatic, and the final printed output can be free from the ubiquitous typex and manual edits that once had to be endured.

Through the use of wordprocessing, moreover, standard documents can be stored for subsequent editing and re-use, cutting down on operator time at every re-draft.

The Development of Wordprocessing

The original generation of wordprocessors used special purpose hardware, dedicated to wordprocessing. However, the various components of the system, screen, keyboard, disks, and so on, are the same in principle as those of the personal computer. Today, there is no reason to use such a specialised machine, in preference to the much more flexible PC.

Since the early days of the microcomputer wordprocessing packages have been available. These were once regarded as poor relations of the dedicated wordprocessor with its specialy configured keys that left little room for operator error, or forgotten key strokes. By comparison, WordStar™, as originally implemented on CP/M machines, was far from user-friendly.

Ability to work in the Total PC Environment

Today's wordprocessing packages are extremely powerful, and generally emulate dedicated wordprocessing systems very closely. Indeed, they improve upon the latter, because of the facility of linking to other PC software: databases, spreadsheets, names and addresses lists and more recently to desk top publishing. Wordprocessing today does not merely speed up the physical process of typing: it makes the whole task of document creation more rapid, efficient and effective.

For this reason, organisations should normally be far better advised to select equipment such as the PC, which offers the ability to process words, and data, keep records or appointments, enable electronic communication; in short provide general personal computing. We should hence regard wordprocessing not as a piece of hardware, but as a software option capable of running on every home and business computer.

Basic Wordprocessing Functions

All the widely accepted wordprocessing packages today are expected to offer certain basic functions. Making the statement, however, is easier than arriving at a list of precisely what these function are. As a starting point, we have taken the features included in the current version of WordStar™, (the all-time de facto leader in PC wordprocessing software) which may be considered as a yardstick for comparison purposes.

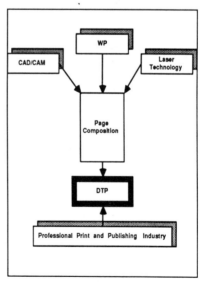

Fig. 3.6   Page layout under PageMaker.

Page formatting

All column guides, margins, gutters, etc. can be specified in inches, millimetres, or picas and points. Ruler guides are available to allow precise placing of headlines, graphics and half tones. Text automatically rewraps upon the changing of column widths.

Typographic features

Kerning (letterspacing), automatic pair kerning, and manual kerning in positive and negative increments are available. The former is predefined according to the manufacturer of the font used, and means quite simply that certain combinations of letters will be differently spaced than others.

Hyphenation and justification

Hyphenation and justification allow for greater aesthetic finish to a document, and are more in keeping with professional typographic standards. PageMaker offers three levels of word spacing for justified text, in addition to flexible hyphenation. A 90,000 word dictionary is provided to cope with auto-hyphenation. Supplied by Houghton Mifflin, the dictionary stipulates the acceptable points at which a word can be hyphenated, hence avoiding unprofessional results in the event that words such as manslaughter or legend be hyphenated inappropriately. Users can add up to 1000 words to the dictionary and will, in addition, be prompted to hyphenate manually any words that are not included. The dictionary cannot be modified, since it is supplied in compressed form. It can, however, be turned off.

In order to fit words on a line, PageMaker runs through the following procedures. Firstly, it tries optimum word spacing, calling on the dictionary to hyphenate the last word in the line if possible. In the event that this fails, minimum word spacing is tried, with recourse to maximum spacing if letterspacing is permitted. The last resort is to hyphenate manually.

Despite sounding complicated, the exercise is in fact transparent to the user, apart from the last step, when a manual hyphenation prompt will appear. In effect, an inter-word spacing range is predetermined, and if PageMaker can not sort out a line within those parameters, the operator is forced to take over. This is an example of the power of the software associated with desktop publishing, and shows how previously skilled tasks can now be done automatically.

Leading

While PageMaker will always default to the leading appropriate to the point size in use, this can be adjusted manually. The facility is of particular use should a portion of text not quite fit into an allotted space. Leading can be altered to close the lines of text together (or indeed move them further apart) so that a perfect fit is achieved.

Graphics/scanned image support

In addition to accepting documents created under traditional Macintosh graphics software (MacDraw, FullPaint, Cricket Graph, Jazz, etc.), files can also be developed using the PostScript language, for subsequent insertion in the document. All graphics images can be scaled to fit allocated space. Additionally, the facility exists to 'crop' a graphic taken from whatever source. Cropping is the act of cutting out a specific part of an image, as opposed to scaling which retains the original in its entirety albeit enlarged or reduced.

PageMaker provides a 'tool box' which contains a number of icons specific to certain functions. Included are basic graphics tools for the creation of lines, boxes and specified fill patterns or shades of grey. Rudimentary graphics can therefore be created directly on screen.

PageMaker supports all files produced on what, in PC terminology, are referred to as 'high resolution scanners' (typically 300 dpi) that use the Tag ImageFile format (TIFF). Examples include Microtek, DEST and Datacopy scanners.

Document production

Unlike earlier releases, PageMaker version 2.0 can create documents of up to 128 pages in length. However, bearing in mind that PageMaker is page-based as oppposed to document-based and is thus not geared to typical long run productions such as manuals, books, etc., the page constraint has never been a real obstacle.

Master pages

PageMaker does not support any style sheet or macro facility. However, it is possible to set up 'master pages' which retain a predefined format throughout the document. Margins and columns can be predetermined, as can headers, footers, boxes, shaded areas, rules, etc. Left and right pages can hold distinct formats.

Page description language (PDL)

PageMaker offers PostScript support, enabling use not only with the Apple LaserWriter but with other high-resolution PostScript-compatible typesetting devices. Graphics files written in PostScript can be placed in PageMaker, and cropped or scaled accordingly. Post-Script files developed in this way can be viewed only when placed on the page.

It is very difficult to go wrong using PageMaker. The same file can be placed, deleted and replaced ad infinitum, since one is using not the original but merely a copy. Changes, amendments, and alterations can be made simply and easily. Indeed, it is amazing how quickly a complicated page can be put together. It is perhaps less amazing how the total flexibility of text manipulation, coupled with the simple moving, scaling and cropping of half-tones and line drawings, can produce such aesthetically horrendous results. Amateur paste-up artists beware: remember that the easiest part of the whole process is learning to use PageMaker! Design skills cannot be acquired overnight.

Manhatten Graphics Ready Set Go 3 – page-based

Thankfully, Ready Set Go 3 bears very little resemblence to either Ready Set Go 1 or 2. The latest release is recognised as a serious rival to PageMaker, and indeed fulfils much the same purpose. Recent endorsement of the product by Letraset, who have adopted it in preference to Boston Software's MacPublisher II, can only serve to create greater credibility and acceptance in the marketplace. What makes Ready Set Go 3 unique is its ability to double as a wordprocessor, an option not normally found with page make-up software.

Text manipulation/page formatting

Ready Set Go 3 offers standard wordprocessing functions, and allows text entry as the page is being made up. Wordprocessing facilities include search and replace, glossary options and a 60,000 word spelling checker.

Ready Set Go 3 pages are composed of text frames (or blocks), graphics frames and ruled lines. Text is keyed directly into the former which can be linked to allow text flow from one to another. Text changes throughout the document, additions or deletions, result in an automatic reflow of text through the linked frames.

Like PageMaker, Ready Set Go 3 offers five preview and edit modes: double size for fine editing, actual size, half page, full page and facing pages. Text runaround, or the flowing of text around a graphic, occurs automatically if text and graphics frames are manipulated so that they overlap.

The concept of building up a series of connected or overlapping text and graphics boxes allows considerable flexibility in layout. Dropped caps, for example, can be achieved by placing the large character in a text frame and positioning this adjacent to the initial paragraph.

Custom rulers specified in inches, centimetres, or picas and points can define page size and layout. In addition, design grids allowing column numbers and formats can be modified to precise requirements. The use of grids enables use of the 'snap to guide' function, for accurate positioning of text and graphics. Point size can be user controlled, i.e. one can overide the defaults supplied with the Macintosh system. Ready Set Go 3 can support anything from 6 to 255 point. We have yet to find a use for the latter!

File import
Ready Set Go 3 offers file import facilities. It is therefore not mandatory to use the program for text entry. Indeed, except in very small organisations, it is unlikely that the person performing the page make-up function will also be keying in copy. MacWrite, Microsoft Word and standard ASCII files can be directly read in. No file export facilities are available.

Kerning
Font-based pair kerning and manual kerning in one point increments are supported.

Hyphenation and justification
Hyphenation is controlled by means of a linguistic-based algorithm, and can be turned on or off for a predefined section of text. If the algorithm is switched on, hyphenation and justification occur at the same rate as standard word wrap. Hyphenation and justification will be correctly and rapidly readjusted through all linked text frames in the event of textual alterations and edits.

Leading
Ready Set Go 3 makes use of automatic leading to point size conventions; manual leading can be specified in half-point increments.

Graphics/scanned image support
MacDraw and MacPaint images can be imported directly into Ready Set Go 3, where they can be scaled or cropped. By extension, any scanned output file supporting the TIFF convention can be imported into MacPaint, and thereafter into Ready Set Go 3, as a bit-mapped graphic.

Master pages/style sheets
Ready Set Go 3, like PageMaker, is page-based. We are beginning to witness the emergence of page-based make-up packages with facilities for long run documents, which hence offer the best of both worlds.

Like PageMaker, Ready Set Go 3 allows the creation of master pages, such that formatting – headers, footers and even the positioning of text and graphics frames – can be set up for odd and even pages, and carried through the document.

In practice, the typical page based document – a newsletter, magazine or even a fairly basic report – will not adhere to a standard format regarding the positioning of line drawings and text on every page. While the master page option therefore has limited usefulness, the notion of linked text frames has far more significance. Changes made to font, point size and style are reflected throughout the entire area of linked text.

PDL
Adobe's PostScript is supported, as is the facility for embedding PostScript code directly into the document in order to achieve a variety of 'special effects'. Sophisticated pages can be produced without recourse to PostScript. This merely reinforces the view that any page make-up package offering PDL support can be enhanced and is less likely to be 'outgrown'. It follows that Ready Set Go 3 can drive the LaserWriter and any other device with a PostScript raster image processor (RIP).

Ease of use
Ready Set Go 3 is a WYSIWYG package that conforms to the standard Macintosh operating procedures. The use of text and graphics frames, while less simple to grasp initially than the Page-Maker system of flexible columns, does have advantages. The speed with which text can be reformatted with simultaneous hyphenation and justification makes for very fast operation.

Ready Set Go 3 version 2.0 offers some interesting facilities: runaround of text, the ability to have several documents open at one time, and cut-and-paste between them is also useful.

Manhattan Graphics has obviously followed PageMaker's lead in incorporating more sophisticated typographical functions. However, there is still room for improvement in this area.

Knowledge Engineering's Just Text – document-based
Just Text, unlike the majority of Macintosh software, does not operate in a WYSIWYG environment, nor does it adhere to the WIMPs conventions. Indeed, of all Macintosh software, Just Text is possibly the most difficult package to learn and use. It warrants special mention because the package offers typographical precision unsurpassed by

any of the DTP software examined above. The user who is prepared to dedicate a degree of learning time can be assured of greater control over the printed page.

In the absence of WYSIWYG, Just Text uses embedded codes, a concept not alien to the typesetting industry. To the traditional Macintosh user, the notion of not being able to see what one is going to get is daunting. A screen preview facility is available for users of version 1.1, but only one viewing size is permitted. For those with a requirement for long, professionally set documents, particularly if there is continuity of point size and typeface (such as in a book), Just Text appears to be ideal. Written in assembler, the program is extremely fast.

Text manipulation
Like Ready Set Go 3, Just Text offers wordprocessing facilities, but there the similarity ends. It is when you start composing pages that the fun begins! However, many functions can be simplified by the use of a macro facility that assigns commonly used routines to specific keys.

Font, type and style can be controlled by embedded codes, as can font width, both expanded and compressed.

File import
'Text tools' enables MacWrite and Word files to be converted into Just Text format; they may still require editing, since the translation is normally not 100 per cent perfect. Unformatted ASCII files can also be imported.

Page formatting
Any number of columns of varying widths can be specified, as can horizontal and vertical tabs. Left and right offset is provided. Text flows automatically into the predefined columns, moving on to the next column when the page end is encountered. Graphics do not follow this continual flow. If they fill up the entire width of the column, Just Text will merely leapfrog the image and continue.

Pages can be defined as broadsheet, tabloid, A4 and smaller. The PostScript output for each size will be correct, despite the fact that a printer such as the LaserWriter will have to output the finished page in sections. Obviously, Just Text is geared to driving all output devices with a PostScript raster image processor (RIP).

Kerning
Comprehensive kerning options are offered. Customised global pair

kerning can be specified, to override standard defaults; manual kerning on a one-off basis is also possible. Just Text allows very precise negative and positive kerning to one thousandth of a point. Commands can be entered in terms of fractions of a point.

Hyphenation and justification
Automatic and discretionary manual hyphenation are supported. A small exception dictionary may be built up. Columns can be justified, centred, or left or right aligned. Given that the correct embedded codes are entered at the beginning of the document or at the precise place when a format change is required, hyphenation and justification will tend to look after itself, the flow of text pausing only when Just Text is defeated in trying to obtain a 'fit' and calls for operator intervention.

Leading
Very specific control is offered over character and line leading.

Graphics/scanned image support
A utility referred to as 'text tools' controls the import of graphics files from MacPaint. Scanned images from Thunderscan can also be accepted, for conversion into PostScript files. Sadly, there is at present no facility for importing MacDraw images. Basic graphics tools are available, via embedded codes, for the creation of boxes and rules in various widths and patterns.

PDL
Not only does Just Text support Adobe's PostScript: it makes considerable use of it. It is used in two distinct ways. Just Text translates the embedded codes and generates a PostScript listing to be sent down to the printer. This element is transparent to the user. Also, PostScript commands and routines can be embedded in the text to produce a wealth of special, but useful effects. Text can be created on diagonal axes, can be curved, or can encircle an object. These effects require complex algorithmns, and knowledge of programming the postscript language.

Ease of use
It is probably superfluous to expand in more depth on Just Text's user-unfriendliness. As with the pros and cons of any software package, it all comes down to what is required in terms of quality, flexibility and typographical sophistication, what types of publications are to be produced, and what skills are available. Those who have mastered Just

Text find it no more difficult to use than WordStar; it is only in the light of traditional Macintosh products that the package appears so complex.

Just Text is currently used by several newspapers, the most notable being *The New York Times*, *The Wall Street Journal*, and *The Boston Globe*. It is a typesetting software package with a specific orientation towards the professional user and creator of long-run documents, and heralds a demand for higher quality output and greater flexibility over typographical functions. The facts that it is outside the mainstream WYSIWYG environment, and that PostScript offers no user-friendly interface, are not prohibitive but leave room for improvement if a package of this power is to command mass appeal.

Other page make-up software

The following are worthy of mention, though not serious contenders.

Orange Micro's Ragtime is an 'integrated' package offering rudimentary wp, spreadsheet, graphics and page layout. It works on the frame, or box, basis rather than using columns. No kerning, hyphenation or control over inter-word spacing are offered; there is PostScript support. This package is not intended for the serious desktop publisher but it is useful, given the built-in spreadsheet, in the production of financial reports.

Boston Software's MacPublisher was, until recently, Letraset's only desktop publishing package, marketed under the guise of Letrapage. However, enhancements continue to be made which will gear MacPublisher/Letrapage towards the graphics art industry rather than towards standard desktop publishing.

Its facilities remain impressive: page-based, WYSIWYG software operating on the 'frame' principle; auto-hyphenation using extensive word dictionary and algorithm; pair plus manual kerning, the latter in one point increments; vertical and horizontal justification. A table of contents is created automatically. The theoretical limits of Letrapage are claimed to be 1024 pages, containing 1024 text files and the same number of graphics files.

Chapter Four
MS-DOS and Desktop Publishing

There is growing awareness that computers are tools that should be easy to use, rather than items of interest for their own sake. The conviction among professionals is that they wish to perform their jobs as expertly, efficiently and profitably as possible, without becoming bogged down in the complexities of computer operation. The adoption of the personal computer to perform certain tasks is a means to an end.

This is the Macintosh approach, which is now being adopted by other computer manufacturers. The approach has two points:

(1) The 'experts', whatever their trade or profession may be, wish to concentrate their energies on that specific area of expertise, and not the complexities of the machine. Any PC-based solution must therefore perform as a tool enhancing rather than hindering the task in hand. This will become increasingly important as personal computers find their way on to more and more desks. The typical user will then no longer be a full-time typist or computer operator. A manager who uses the screen only occasionally will need to be helped and guided by a visual and friendly approach; otherwise, he may give up using the system. Ease of use and, by extension, a short learning curve is the key.

(2) The nature of PC-based page make-up software is such that it demands, with a few notable exceptions, a WYSIWYG standard that can best be achieved in a WIMPs or Macintosh-like operating environment.

Imitating the Macintosh

Not surprisingly, the impression that the Macintosh has made on the market has given rise to a number of imitations. The closest imitation, in the IBM PC environment, has been Digital Research's GEM suite of software. Unfortunately, Apple were not flattered by the imitation, which was so close that Apple threatened legal action. GEM had to be withdrawn for cosmetic surgery to make its icons less Apple-like.

GEM is not the only product of its class. The main rival to GEM is Microsoft Windows. Other windowing products so far announced have included VisiOn from VisiCorp, Taxi from Epson, and Topview from IBM itself. There is not room for so many contenders in the market, and several of them seem already to have disappeared.

What is GEM?

GEM is actually several different things: a standard method of presenting information to the user, a standard method of dealing with the screen and keyboard, and a series of programs, of which the GEM Desktop is the first one you are likely to use.

When you start up GEM, a 'desktop' appears on the screen, with two windows open. Normally, one of these represents the system as a whole, with several icons already displayed – one for each disk drive you have in your machine. The Desktop program allows you to do everything you could normally do, using MS-DOS commands, but in many cases these commands are triggered by manipulating the icons on the screen rather than typing commands. Generally, in terms of operating procedures, GEM apes the Macintosh way of working.

As well as the GEM Desktop program, there is a variety of GEM application software offering, for example, graphically orientated 'Write' and 'Draw' programs similar to Apple's MacWrite and MacDraw. These programs are specially designed to work with the GEM Desktop, and use the same conventions for the mouse and the opening and moving of windows.

For some computers, such as the Macintosh, the WIMPs type of presentation was introduced right from the start, so that virtually all Macintosh software follows the same conventions. With MS-DOS-based PCs the situation is different, since the majority of software was written to run under MS-DOS without reference to GEM, and so does not use the GEM approach. Once the user exits from the GEM environment, they revert to raw MS-DOS.

GEM Paint
Like MacPaint, GEM Paint is a freehand graphics package, essentially a tool for the illustrator. In other words, GEM Paint gives you the equivalent of a pencil, a ruler and compass, a variety of paints and

paintbrushes, an airbrush, an eraser, and a paint tap which you can turn on to flood an entire area with colour. There is even a microscope, the equivalent of MacPaint's 'Fat Bits', that you can use to focus in on a particular area you wish to work on in fine detail.

In their efforts to avoid Apple's threatened lawsuit, Digital Research have made considerable changes to the nomenclature of features and the design of icons, without losing the benefits that are available with the Macintosh system. These facilities can be used by the desktop publisher.

GEM Draw

As the name suggests, this is GEM's answer to Apple's structured graphics package. GEM Draw offers much the same flexibility, features and functions that are found in MacDraw.

A favourite tool of the graphic designer today is the Letraset sheet of standard symbols (now available in Macintosh format – but more of Letraset later!), to be put on to the page in the appropriate place. The electronic equivalent is the GEM Draw Business Library, which has a whole variety of special borders, organisation templates, electronic circuit symbols, and so on. The Macintosh system offers a plethora of graphics design libraries, including such topics as architecture and landscape gardening, in addition to more general special effects, standard diagrams and forms. These packages, though inexpensive (normally under £50), must be purchased separately. GEM provides a rudimentary library with the total system, from which selections can be copied as required into your GEM Draw diagram to give the whole document a consistent and professional appearance.

GEM Paint and GEM Draw will obviously be compared with the MacPaint and MacDraw programs for the Apple Macintosh. The programs are, in fact, very similar, apart from restrictions imposed by different screen resolutions; on the other hand, the GEM versions are able to work in colour.

GEM Graph

The idea that a picture is worth a thousand words has been applied in business, particularly to the generation of so-called 'business graphics', to bring life to numbers. GEM Graph, like the Macintosh package 'Cricket Graph', can be used either as a stand-alone product or as a vehicle for the output of data from another program.

GEM WordChart

The 'illustrated lecture' was a favourite entertainment in Victorian

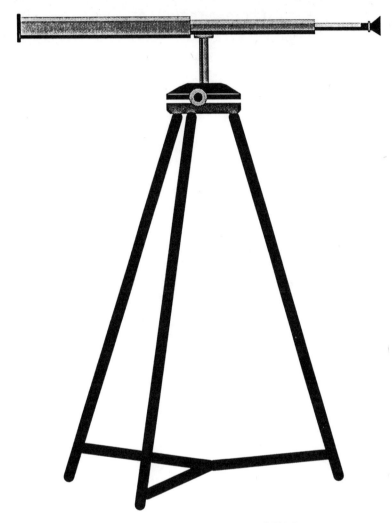

Fig. 4.1 Illustration produced using GEM Draw.

times, when the magic lantern or the epidiascope were the available technology. Today, the overhead projector foil and the 35 millimetre slide are favoured for business presentations. Visual aids can add a great deal to the impact of a talk, but in the past it has been expensive and difficult to produce really professional-looking material.

GEM WordChart is specially designed for this sort of use. It contains a series of templates into which text can be added, so that the text is automatically centred or arranged in columns. A choice of fonts and styles are available, and output in colour is possible. Additionally, the text can be surrounded with plain or decorative borders, produced using either GEM WordChart itself, or perhaps GEM Draw.

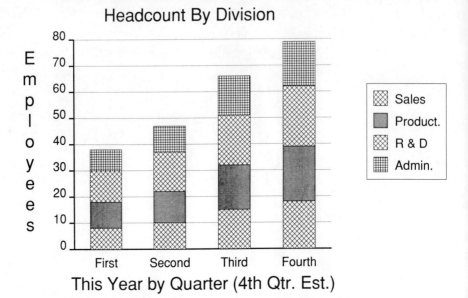

Fig. 4.2 Example of output produced by GEM Graph.

Special typefaces

Much of the impact of good graphic design comes from the careful selection of fonts and typefaces. The GEM fonts and drivers pack comes with a library of different sizes and types of text characters, as well as patterns and sample pictures for use with GEM Paint. Of greatest significance, given our overriding concern with desktop publishing, is the fact that GEM provides PostScript drivers. The optimum output device, if industry standard fonts are to be obtained and full page graphics supported, would be the Apple LaserWriter, or indeed any other PostScript device.

Microsoft Windows

Despite being officially announced in 1984, it was only with the success of desktop publishing on the Macintosh, and the realisation that a similar environment was called for on the IBM PC, that Windows received recognition in the marketplace. Certainly, the decision on the part of Aldus to adopt Windows as the vehicle for their MS-DOS version of PageMaker has helped this process. Moreover, by putting pressure on Microsoft to enhance the product by, for example, building in PostScript drivers, Aldus contributed to its new-found acceptance.

Windows uses considerable storage and processing overhead. Unlike GEM, which runs on the lower-end IBM PCs and compatibles, the minimum workable hardware configuration required by Windows is an AT class machine, i.e. one based on the 80286 chip. Anything less will slow down operation of the application software quite considerably. A perennial problem facing any IBM PC-based desktop publishing system lies in the RAM constraint of 640K imposed by MS-DOS. To overcome this, Windows supports the standard memory expansion solutions now available such as the Lotus/Intel Above board and AST Rampage board which RAM increases up to 2 megabytes.

Windows, acting as an extension to MS-DOS, provides the user with a Macintosh-like interface. Like GEM, however, the environment is limited to those applications that support the user interface.

Application software

Microsoft Windows, like GEM, is supplied with its own suite of application software: Windows Write, Paint and Draw. Basically, these follow the standard conventions of their Macintosh counterparts, and as such do not warrant in-depth examination.

Microsoft is intent on expanding the suite of available software and is looking to other software houses to develop applications written for Windows. To date it has met with little success, other than a few major coups – not least the implementation of Windows-based PageMaker. Other products in the pipeline include a PC publishing package from Micropro, the makers of WordStar, and from Micrografix – the company responsible for the development of Windows Draw – a business graphics package, Windows Graph.

Linking data

In order to enhance the electronic cut-and-paste associated with the WIMPs environment, Microsoft will shortly be releasing its own dynamic data exchange (DDE) protocol for Windows. This will allow linking of data from applications written to run in Windows and support DDE.

We have always found the cut-and-paste feature not only simple and workable but also extremely logical, since it effectively emulates an activity that is recognisable and hence meaningful to the user. What DDE will provide is dynamic data links. In simple terms, this means that any related data, albeit in different files, will be simultaneously updated.

Dynamic data links, while extremely useful in some cases, should be treated with caution. Let us take an example. We link a pie chart produced in Window Graphs to a Write text file to create a financial report. When a new set of figures is released, the pie chart is manually amended to reflect changes. At this point the chart in the financial report is automatically updated which, depending on what was intended, could be a tremendous aid or a major mistake.

Microsoft has also developed a text transfer protocol called 'rich text format (RTF). Like IBM's document control architecture (DCA), RTF accepts text files from other packages without losing formatting, font and typeface changes. Given that many personal computer application packages have already adopted the DCA protocol, is Microsoft confusing the issue by promoting another?

Windowing

One advantage Windows offers over the Macintosh/GEM system is a multi-tasking environment. This allows several applications to be open on screen at one time, permitting the user to jump from one to another. The term 'multi-tasking' can be misleading, since only one application can actually be used at any given moment. The others are, as it were, in stand-by mode: they are loaded and ready, but doing nothing. The only activity that can proceed in background mode is printing.

MS-DOS user interface vs. Macintosh

The primary difference between the two has its foundation in the hardware constraints imposed by the Macintosh or, to look at it another way, the hardware flexibility of MS-DOS-based machines. Despite its clarity and high resolution, the Macintosh screen is monochrome. The IBM PC and compatibles, by virtue of their 'open architecture' design, can support a range of display options. Both GEM and Microsoft Windows make full use of the available colour facilities. This offers certain advantages, not only in the aesthetics of graphics creation, and also serves to simplify the process of colour output.

Colour laser printers are considered well outside the price range of the typical desktop publisher. Colour plotters and dot matrix printers do not meet the required standard of output resolution. In effect, there is no benefit to be gained from using colour display for desktop publishing. The Macintosh, despite its monochrome screen, can output in colour using utilities such as MacPlot, which interprets 'fill' patterns as distinct colours, and MacPalette, which does likewise for ImageWriter colour output. However, using low-cost laser output, one can achieve spot colour only by changing the toner cartridge and running the paper through twice.

GEM and Windows both reside between MS-DOS and the application software. The user is thus denied a consistent environment in which to work. One thing is clear: the GEM and Windows environments have allowed the MS-DOS personal computer to mature into a viable desktop publishing tool.

Desktop publishing software under MS-DOS

Page composition software is nothing new to the IBM PC. Prefis' Book Machine and PagePlanner have been around for several years. They were basically text-only packages, offering relatively precise typographical features combined with columnar layouts – a rare facility at the time. The real impediments to their success lay in the lack of any high-resolution yet low-cost output device, in the prohibitive cost (£2000 +), and in the fundamental fact that the desktop publishing revolution had not yet occurred. Prefis wisely sat back and waited for laser technology to make quantum leaps, and for market awareness to develop. It has now enhanced its existing software to an acceptable desktop publishing standard, which we will examine below.

It was only in the latter part of 1986 that MS-DOS-based page make-up packages able to conform to true desktop publishing criteria emerged. Even then, many were still at the 'vapourware' stage: we had all heard about them, magazines had reviewed them (often incorrectly – probably as a result of not having access to them), but you couldn't actually purchase them. Where were they?

The quality and choice of page make-up software for the IBM PC and compatibles that became available almost overnight was astounding. The majority of current IBM PC-compatible desktop publishing software was announced at the Seybold Conference held in San Francisco in September 1986. Hence the sudden surge of products. It was therefore not surprising when the same pattern was repeated in the UK in January 1987. A European re-run of the San Francisco conference launched a wealth of products and generated a level of interest and demand that could not be immediately satisfied.

Three products in particular have emerged as clear market leaders in the US: Aldus PageMaker, Xerox's Ventura Publisher and Harvard Professional Publisher. UK trends to date appear to be following US developments closely, and we have therefore concentrated on a close examination of the three packages mentioned above. Attention will also be given to products that, for reasons of their origins or specialised appeal, also warrant inclusion.

Aldus PageMaker – page-based

The success of PageMaker on the Macintosh, due in part to Apple's enthusiastic endorsement of the product, has been astounding. However, while Apple's promotion undoubtedly boosted PageMaker sales, the reverse is also true; it is reckoned that one in three of installed Macintoshes, excluding pre-PageMaker/LaserWriter product availability, were primarily purchased to use PageMaker. Our experience tends to support this. That PageMaker is currently the de facto leader in desktop publishing software is uncontested; it has the world's largest installed base, is available in eight languages, and is said to hold 90 per cent of market share in the US. It was an obvious move, therefore, to offer the world's leading desktop publishing package on the worlds leading PC!

Early on, Aldus planned to use Microsoft Windows as the interface vehicle with which to break into the PC market. However, modifications were obviously required since, despite Windows' apparent similarity to the Macintosh, the former is very different in architecture and more complex for the programmer to work with. In order to make optimum use of the strong features of the two environments, Aldus completely rewrote the package (using 'C') to run under both systems.

PageMaker version 1.0 for the IBM offers the same functions and features as the Macintosh version 2.0 outlined above. Indeed, once loaded on the PC, it is almost impossible for the user to tell the difference between the two. It is therefore superfluous to itemise again the characteristics of the package. The key difference lies in the lack of uniformity of IBM PC software. One cannot simply cut-and-paste text and graphics from one software package to another; therefore we need to examine the type of data that can be accepted by PageMaker.

File import
Text and graphics can be imported by using the now familiar 'place' command. IBM's DCA (document content architecture) is fully

supported, hence type characteristics and formatting will not be lost in transfer. The following programs are supported:

Word processors
- Windows Write
- Microsoft Word
- WordStar 3.3
- Multimate
- XYWrite
- ASCII text files
- DCA format files

Graphics
- Windows Paint and Draw
- PC Paint
- PC Paintbrush
- AutoCAD
- Lotus 1-2-3 and Symphony
- TIFF files

Microsoft Windows is not supplied with PageMaker; a copy must therefore be purchased prior to using the software.

Xerox Ventura Publisher – document based

Ironically, it is due to Xerox that desktop publishing ever emerged at all: firstly, with the development of SmallTalk that formed the basis of the Lisa and Macintosh WIMPs environment, and secondly, with initial work in the field of page description languages that led ultimately to Adobe's PostScript and to Xerox's own imPRESS.

Despite offering the Documenter – a complete desktop publishing system – Xerox, realising the potential of the IBM-installed base, chose to market a software product aimed exclusively at the IBM PC market. The resulting program, Ventura Publisher – developed by Ventura Software – is tending to detract from Documenter, and is not boosting Xerox laser printer sales (the preferred printer continues to be the Apple LaserWriter).

User interface
Ventura is supplied with a 'run time' version of Digital Research's GEM. This means that GEM does not have to be purchased separately. It is not, however, a full-blown version, but merely the

GEM Desktop which serves to provide the required WIMPs/ WYSIWYG environment. Keyboard shortcuts are provided through the use of control keys.

Ventura Software opted for GEM in preference to Windows for the simple reason that the developers came from a Digital Research background. The GEM environment allows more support for lower specification machines than does Windows, and could therefore be advantageous for the existing PC user.

Text manipulation

Like PageMaker, Ventura offers limited text editing and is geared for page make-up using previously created text files. Once again, the advantage in this approach lies in the opportunity for users to continue using preferred, existing wp software. Text files, depending on their origin, can be imported with character attributes intact, or transferred in straight ASCII format. Supported wordprocessors, i.e. those offering the former transfer facilities, include:

- Microsoft Word
- WordPerfect
- Windows Write
- GEM Write
- Multimate
- WordStar

Letters, words and blocks of text can be specified in or changed to bold, italic, small caps, strikethrough, all caps, all lower case, subscript, superscript and underline.

Using the text mode, editing can be performed at any stage. Four viewing levels are supported: 100 per cent (actual size), 50 per cent, 200 per cent and facing pages. Real time reformatting occurs as text is edited, hence a deletion in one line will cause all remaining text to be automatically hyphenated and formatted. If a graphic is encountered during the flow, the text will merely run around the obstructing image.

Page formatting

Ventura operates in four program modes: frames, paragraph tag, text and graphics. The formatting of pages works on the basis of creating distinct frames intended to accept graphics or text. The paragraph tag facility allows definition of a specific paragraph's format by assigning font size, type, indentation, leading and text alignment.

Up to eight various width columns can be set up per page or frame. Verso (left) and recto (right) pages can be formatted independently.

Headers, footers and automatic page numbering are supported. The latter can be specified in Arabic, Roman, or numbers spelled out.

Five page sizes can be defined including A4, B5 and American quarto.

Typographical features

Automatic hyphenation and justification (H&J), if specified, occurs without operator intervention as text is flowed into frames or edited. Leading control in fractional point sizes is supported. Dropped caps and vertical and horizontal tabs are also featured.

Graphics/scanned image support

In common with the all WYSIWYG make-up systems, limited graphics tools are supplied to add aesthetic finish to documents. Lines, boxes and circles of various thickness can be drawn directly on to the page. Graphics generated by the following software can be played directly into frames using the graphics mode:

- AutoCAD
- GEMDraw
- GEM Graph
- GEM Paint
- PC Paintbrush
- Lotus 1-2-3 and Symphony
- CAD DXF (data exchange format) files
- TIFF files

Graphics, once imported, can be repositioned or scaled to size.

Document length

Ventura is orientated towards production of long documents such as books, manuals, etc. Chapter size is dictated by RAM constraints. Up to 64 chapters can be linked together in one document. Page counter provides numbering from 1 to 9999. Automatic table of contents and index generation support Ventura's emphasis on the long-run publication.

Master pages/style sheets

Control over document format is accommodated by the use of style sheets. User-created 'tags' define the format of all text or of one paragraph. Each tag is named and can subsequently be stored for reuse. The collection of tags used in one document is saved as a style sheet. Features regulated under the tag system include the typographical functions outlined above, character attributes, and standard page formatting specifications such as margins, columns, page breaks and control over widows and orphans. In addition, indents, paragraph spacing and text alignment can all be specified.

Tag names can be embedded directly into a wordprocessed document, or assigned directly to paragraphs in Ventura. Once tag mode is selected, a directory of existing tags appears on screen, text is selected and the appropriate specification attached. Tag characteristics can be amended at any stage, so that all text assigned to that specific style will reflect the changes. This facility provides a simple method of making overall changes to, say, point size throughout the document.

For the benefit of the inexperienced desktop publisher, Ventura is supplied with a library of predefined style sheets. As discussed above, the most difficult aspect of page make-up for the first-time user is not getting to grips with the software but mastering standard layout conventions. The addition of sample style sheets for such publications as newsletters, books and product lists provides the uninitiated with guidelines for the creation of professional-looking publications.

PDL support
Ventura supports the PostScript page description language, and has incorporated DDL drivers. The package also offers a variety of Bitstream downloadable fonts for use with Hewlett-Packard LaserJet printers. Typefaces, over and above the standard Times and Helvetica, include Avant Garde, Bookman, Optima and Palatino. Width tables, stored in memory, must be specified for each font used; by implication, the more fonts used in one document, the less memory will be available.

The PostScript font width table can be loaded to allow use of the Hewlett-Packard as a proofing device for PostScript typesetting devices. This will ensure that each character/word/line claims the same amount of space as it should under industry standard typeface conventions. Obviously, the simplest way of ensuring true output would be to drive a PostScript laser printer from day one.

Ease of use

Ventura is supplied on eleven disks – which can initially be a little daunting. A significant amount of the 3 megabytes of program is dedicated to printer drivers (of which there are many), down loadable fonts, and font width tables. Under most circumstances, the user would not need to load all the disks to get started. Given that Ventura

Publisher operates in the Windows/GEM environment, it is by implication relatively simple to learn and use.

Getting to grips with the basic operational modes – text, graphics, frames, and paragraph tag – is perhaps the least demanding aspect of working with this program. The printing options, typographical functions and creation of style sheets may prove less obvious to the first time publisher. The documentation supplied is good, however, and a comprehensive tutorial section is supplied.

Ventura adheres to the concept of dynamically linked files. Changes in the original will be reflected in the publication.

In the desktop publishing market, Ventura is considered to be the package able to pose a real challenge to PageMaker's current supremacy. The two packages, however, are orientated towards slightly different target users, the former being admirably suited to the production of long-run publications and the latter clearly geared to flexible design of pages such as might be used in newsletters, advertising copy, product briefs, flyers, etc. If this is correct and the potential for desktop publishing is as significant as we believe it to be (by the end of the decade it is reckoned that three billion pages of information will be published by businesses worldwide), there is surely room for at least two leading software solutions. Competition can only benefit the publisher who will surely use the enhancements resulting from software vendor 'one-upmanship' to advantage.

Bestinfo's Harvard Professional Publisher – page-based, with document facilities

Marketed by Software Publishing Corporation, Bestinfo's HPP is primarily in the PageMaker vein, with the addition of a style sheet facility. While less dedicated in application than either Ventura or PageMaker, HPP offers general purpose desktop publishing yet provides sophisticated typographical features and PostScript drivers. An unusual aspect of HPP is that it uses neither Windows nor GEM as a user interface; the program runs directly under MS-DOS, and as such can operate on a standard hard disk PC. As always, for desktop publishing applications a 286 or superior machine is recommended.

By not adopting an existing WIMPs environment to base HPP, Bestinfo have enabled the program to consume less RAM and disk space, but in so doing have, in effect, reinvented the wheel, since HPP operates in a WYSIWYG mode.

HPP's advantage in competition with the evergrowing plethora of

IBM-based packages is twofold. Harvard Presentation Graphics, from the same source, has a sound reputation and a well established base among IBM PC users. Moreover, Professional Publisher derives from Bestinfo's SuperPage II, of which it is basically a rewrite, though much less sophisticated, aimed at a larger audience and hence offered at lower cost. SuperPage II, also available on the IBM PC, handles the entire pre-press production process, including text entry, page composition and output through a selection of over 25 typesetting devices. At approximately £7000 SuperPage II cannot realistically be subsumed within the category of desktop publishing.

Text manipulation

HPP offers limited wordprocessing capabilities (i.e. the facility for restricted on-screen text editing, which automatically updates all other text), and is, in the main, dependent on text import from other sources. Any wordprocessing packages able to ouput in ASCII or DCA file format, plus any spreadsheet print file, can be accepted. Pages can be reviewed using HPP's zoom facility at the following levels, 200 per cent actual size, one page or facing pages.

In addition to the standard typeface styles – bold, italic, etc. – type can be expanded, condensed or reversed (white on black). Dropped caps can be specified.

Page formatting

Multiple columns, automatic page numbering, headers and footers, alignment of lists and tables, and continuation messages are all supported. Any number of master page formats can be used within one document. Text can be flowed page by page, or throughout the entire document. Widow and orphan control (i.e. the ability to specify paragraph breaks over columns or pages) is permitted.

Typographical features

Automatic pair kerning and tracking (i.e. the automatic reduction of spacing between characters and words in a given line) is supported.

Text is automatically hyphenated and justified (if specified) as it is flowed into the document. Hyphenation is controlled by means of an algorithm supported by a dictionary. Manual hyphenation is possible, and may prove necessary as no exception dictionary is supplied. HPP attempts to obtain word fit through wordspacing and letter spacing facilities.

Graphics/scanned input
HPP accepts graphics files generated under the following software:

- Harvard Presentation Graphics
- Lotus 1-2-3
- PC Paintbrush
- Windows Paint
- PC Paint Plus
- TIFF files from high-resolution scanners

Once accepted, graphic images can be scaled or cropped. Standard rudimentary graphics tools are supplied for the creation of rules and boxes; the latter can be filled with varying grey scale tints to produce special effects/mark areas for subsequent pasting of half-tones, in the event that scanned input is not deemed acceptable. Text performs automatic runaround when an irregular image is encountered.

Master pages/style sheets
Long documents can be preformatted using the style sheet option. Global changes can be effected throughout the document merely by amending the attached style sheet. Piping, or the flowing of text on to many pages, assists in this process. Shorter or single-page documents can most efficiently be altered using on-screen editing.

PDL and Harvard Professional Publisher
Harvard Professional Publisher supports all PostScript devices. Bit-mapped output is not supported but, as mentioned above, we are not overly concerned with dot matrix output other than for checking text at the pre make-up stage. Given that Hewlett-Packard LaserJet drivers are also supplied, it seems likely that DDL will be supported in the near future.

Ease of use
HPP is not as simple to set up, nor as logical to work with, as PageMaker. The decision to conform to the preferred WYSIWYG operating environment obviously implies a certain ease of use. We found text editing frustrating, in so far as a dynamic link with the original text file meant we were restricted to editing portions of text within a frame and not as laid out on the page. We also had difficulty locating the piece of text to be edited, having to scroll through the frame to find the precise letter or word to be changed. This may not irritate the first-time user, but those accustomed to page, as opposed to window, editing may find it a definite drawback.

Other desktop publishing packages

It would be impossible to cover all available IBM PC-based page make-up and composition software in such depth. We have extracted the salient features of a cross section of 'the others', in an attempt to define the current state of the market. Other contenders include the following.

Studio Software's Front Page/Front Page Plus – page-based layout system, using frame concept

Boxes are drawn on screen, and text flowed in. Most common typographic features are supported; mainly WYSIWYG, though some operations require the user to insert composition parameters into raw text file. Recomposition into WYSIWYG form is slow. Despite good documentation, this package is less easy to use than most desktop publishing software. Twelve boards (style sheets) are supplied – helpful to the novice desktop publisher – with the standard version. Front Page Plus offers a macro facility which allows the set-up of bespoke style sheets, and more sophisticated features. Both packages offer PostScript support. Software add-ons in the form of typesetter drivers (Linotype, Compugraphic) can be purchased, as can a typographer's utility program, to allow for the setting up of width tables. Despite page-based layout, the macro facility under Front Page Plus makes it ideal for the long-run publication.

Mirrorsoft's Fleet Street Editor and Fleet Street Publisher

Mirrorsoft, originally part of the Mirror Newspaper Group, first developed Fleet Street Editor to run on the BBC Micro for the educational market. It is now implemented on the IBM PC and Amstrad CPC and PCW range. FSE and FSP are WYSIWYG packages operating on a linked text box principle and offering adequate typographical features, given a very low price (under £200). Text can be keyed in directly, and any ASCII wordprocessed file is accepted. Standard graphics facilities are supported in terms of cropping and scaling, and also the import of graphic screens (using a 'snap shot' feature), not graphic files. They come supplied with a library of graphic images.

Fleet Street Editor represents an ideal starting point for the less ambitious desktop publisher. The number of columns is limited to four; both 'bastard' (of unequal width) and standard are allowed. PostScript drivers are available. Fleet Street Publisher offers more sophisticated typographical features, and page formatting controls.

The emergence of standards

The software packages outlined above point clearly to the emergence of certain standards. All support some form of user interface, and operate in a WYSIWYG environment. We have omitted those that:

(a) Do not offer PostScript or some other industry acceptable page description language and, by extension, cannot output the made-up page directly to a typesetter.

(b) Are no more than glorified wordprocessing systems, lacking the typographical functions considered essential for page make-up.

(c) Are still at the 'vapourware' or beta testing stage.

Lastly, some of the most powerful software packages around are those that do not conform to WIMP conventions and cannot be said to offer a true WYSIWYG facility. Despite that, they are significant in the development of low-cost systems that offer viable typesetting front-end capabilities. Software of this nature is more common under DOS, and in many cases has been available since long before the desktop publishing revolution was conceived.

Chapter Five
Multi-user Desktop Publishing

Such is the power and flexibility of the personal computer that it is tempting for desktop publishers to think it is the only computer they would require. In fact, of course, a single-user micro is not the answer to every computer need. There is often a place for bigger and more powerful computers, although in many cases the personal computer still fits into the picture as a terminal or workstation.

Multi-user systems

The main reason for choosing a bigger machine is that a multi-user system is required. Of course, a network of personal computers can sometimes be an alternative to a multi-user computer, but if there is a need to share data and processing power – for instance, when a number of authors are producing one document, or a large database has to be shared among many users – then a multi-user system could well be the most effective solution.

It is possible to use the IBM-PC-type machine for multi-user working, under XENIX, UNIX or PICK; but there will be a need for bigger disks, bigger memory, and a more powerful processor than the personal computer can provide. These multi-user machines come in many sizes and can be classified under a number of headings. Most of the machines fall into one of three categories:

- Mainframe computers, particularly the IBM machines and the plug-compatibles
- Minicomputers, particularly the DEC VAX range
- A variety of minis and supermicros running UNIX and PICK

The machines that can be subsumed under the multi-user desktop publishing banner are the latter: supermicros running UNIX.

Local area networks

A local area network (LAN) is a group of workstations (PCs) controlled by a central file server – generally a more powerful model of the same type – and connected in one of two ways. Either they can be linked in a star formation, each PC communicating independently with the controller; or, conversely, each constituent machine on the network can be daisychained in a ring formation. A LAN is more than the sum total of a collection of PCs linked by cables. It necessitates the use of sophisticated software, and the addition of controller boards to each participating PC, in order to manage the constant demands made on the central hard disk or file server. The type of network system adopted will in turn dictate the composition and arrangement of the PCs.

The software that enables a group of PCs to work together from a central file serving device also ensures certain levels of file security. This prevents, for example, two users unwittingly editing the same document simultaneously. Networks can reduce overall equipment costs quite considerably by permitting several users to share storage devices and printers. AppleTalk, Apple's rudimentary but efficient peripheral sharing LAN, achieves precisely this cost saving.

LANs for the IBM PC and compatibles are at a more sophisticated level of development, and would prove ideal vehicles for the desktop publisher. The benefit of the LAN approach lies in providing individual users with access to the same document, in order to perform their discrete function in the publishing process. Examples of popular LANs include Torus, which makes use of a WIMP-like user interface, Novell Netware and IBM's Token Ring.

Eddie Shah opts for networked PCs

One example of networked personal computers in a publishing environment results from Eddie Shah's descision to implement new systems at both the Stockport Messenger and Warrington Guardian Groups. The installed hardware consists of Macintoshes linked by AppleTalk running under the AppleShare file server software, which allows files to be passed from one user to another. Talbot Dialtext Editorial Software performs all text inputting and composition functions, and allows reformatting to a predefined standard at the editorial stage. Quite simply, format codes are applied and typeset copy is generated.

Collectively, the Messenger and the Warrington Guardian groups are operating with 86 Macintosh workstations, spread over 14 sites. Shah is said to have saved over £1 million by rejecting the Hastech system adopted for production of the *Today* newspaper.

The single vs. the multi-user environment

The difference between desktop publishing on a supermicro running UNIX and the desktop publishing systems mentioned so far is, in essence, the difference between single and multi-user systems. There are certain cases when a multi-user or networked system will be more effective. One such case is office automation, where the desktop publishing system is an integral part of the office system. The terminals or workstations could be used as wordprocessing stations, or telex teminals, or data entry terminals.

The multi-user set-up would have different software running on the system – not all of which would interface with the desktop publishing. One very large example is the system in the US Department of Defense which has thousands of terminals linked to a number of supermicros running UNIX. They are used to handle all the routine office automation requirements as well as publishing many of the thousands of documents concerned with commands and equipment specifications used by the Department.

Criteria for a multi-user system

There are a number of reasons for providing a multi-user environment. These include:

- To share computer power
- To share the benefits of expensive peripherals such as scanners, digitisers and laser printers
- To share data and text files
- To allow users overall communication with others on the system

Sharing processing power
Before the advent of inexpensive processing power in the form of personal computing, there was a need to reduce the cost of a system by maximising the sharing of processing power. Mainframes and minis able to support multiple users were thus the most commonly adopted

computer solution. However, as the price of processing power decreased, so the need to distribute it between users became less acute. Indeed, in many cases it became more cost effective to provide single users with their own PCs.

The Multi-user computers still have their place for certain types of application involving centralised processing. In many situations, there is a need for a powerful machine at the centre, essentially as a file server, with a large disk holding common files.

Sharing peripherals

In the desktop publishing environment, sharing peripherals can be important. This does not apply, of course, to matrix printers, which are now so cheap that it is not worth the cost of providing a multi-user system to allow them to be shared – it is cheaper to give a printer to each user. However, the state of affairs has not yet arrived in which laser printers and digitisers can be provided locally for everyone. They are expensive items, and are likely to remain so for some time to come.

Sharing data and files

The sharing of data and text files is a more fundamental need, and one more difficult to fulfil. Nonetheless, whenever several users need to access the same data, it can be dangerous for them to have their own copies, as the different copies may get out of step. Files therefore need to be shared.

This is essential in operations where more than one user will need to access the same document/file, albeit at different times and for diverse purposes. To put this in perspective, user A enters copy, user B edits and alters copy and user C makes up a page, having accessed the graphics file produced by user D. User E proofs and checks the final page before output. At any stage in the process, the document is accessible from the central file server; and while file security protocols must operate, so that one file cannot be updated by several people simultaneously, this method of working saves a lot of leg work!

The main problem with sharing data arises when several people do try to update the same data at the same time. This can easily lead to the data becoming corrupted. It is, therefore, essential to provide some means of 'locking', so that if a particular record is being amended it is locked and cannot be accessed by anyone else, other than for viewing, until the update is completed. The UNIX operating system allows this.

For the purposes of this exercise, the UNIX operating structure allows files to be assigned as 'read only' (ro), or 'read/write' (rw). Assignments can be amended only by the system housekeeper or, in the case of private files, by the originator. Moreover, the status of a file may differ from user to user, a system maintained through the use of passwords. This ensures absolute security of data, while permitting many users access to documents under controlled conditions.

Electronic mail
The final reason for providing a multi-user environment is to enable different office workers and desktop publishers to communicate with each other. The key activity here is electronic messaging, or electronic mail.

When a number of people from different departments are producing a desktop-published document, it is useful and effective if they can send parts of the document to each other by electronic mail. The editor also has an easier time since texts from different contributors can be obtained from a central source and combined. This is the way in which a number of newspapers are produced.

Refinements to UNIX-based desktop publishing software are needed. Despite a wealth of graphics software available under UNIX, there is as yet little available in the way of desktop publishing packages. The hardware, however, is ideal, and the traditional graphics orientation has led to the development of UNIX-based graphics workstations, offering a resolution suitable for the desktop publishing environment.

Troff (Typesetting RunOff)

One of the first supermicro-based publishing systems is 'troff', a program within the UNIX operating system. It is available as a formatting utility, forming part of AT&T's powerful document preparation tools collectively referred to as the 'documenter's workbench'.

The standard UNIX screen editor, vi, is a development of ed, which originated in the pre-VDU teletype days, and as such offered non-interactive editing and no screen representation of the text. Vi offered improvements over this. The document formatters, by extension, evolved from the same hardware constraints, and are thus, to coin a jargon phrase, of the YCNSWYG (you can not see what you'll get) type.

Troff, constituting the major formatter, was designed to produce high-quality output on a typesetter. Multiple fonts and point sizes are supported, in addition to facilities such as paragraph styles, headings, footnotes, etc. Troff can also output directly to laser printers. Given that troff cannot support a WYSIWYG style, text is first prepared with embedded formatting commands under vi.

Several powerful pre-processors extend the capabilities of troff – eqn, tbl, pic and grap – by providing layout facilities for equations, tables, graphics and graphs respectively.

Troff is not used often now because, despite exceptional power and flexibility, it is understandably very difficult to master. Indeed, it is not unknown for grown men to be reduced to tears when trying to produce documents using this system.

SoftQuad Publishing software (Unixsys UK)

SoftQuad claims to provide 'troff without tears'. An enhanced derivation of AT&T's documentor workbench, it combines the power of troff with considerably more ease of use. Its appeal to existing UNIX users lies in the fact that it can accept any standard troff files.

SoftQuad's salient features include:-

- A preview facility of any formatted page and document
- As an extension to troff, SoftQuad is a document-based composition package; simple reformatting of entire documents can be achieved merely by making changes to one formatting file
- Macro formatting tools allow programmers to develop specific in-house format requirements

Typographical features
Hyphenation and justification is fully supported; the original AT&T hyphenation algorithm is used, supported by an exception dictionary. Kerning is dealt with through the use of software supplied to generate kerning tables for fonts found on the target output device.

File import facilities
SoftQuad can accept and reformat files produced under non-UNIX software, including output from wordprocessors, spreadsheets and databases.

Graphics support
Supplied with SoftQuad are tools for the generation of charts, diagrams and graphs. Tables can be laid out as required, and the creation of boxes and rules is supported.

PDL support

SoftQuad supports the PostScript PDL, and can thus drive the Apple LaserWriter, the Linotype 100 and 300 phototypesetters, and indeed any other PostScript device. Transcript and imPRESS, other supported PDLs (or intermediate languages in UNIX parlance), increase the range of output devices that can be driven.

Hardware considerations

SoftQuad Publishing software is available on standard UNIX-based machines running the following varients of UNIX: version 7, Berkeley 4.2, System V and Xenix. These include IBM PC XT and AT, Olivetti PCs, Pyramid, Sun, Apollo, the AT&T 3B range, and the DEC VAX and PDP 11 machines, to mention but a few. SoftQuad can cost anything between £700 and £20,000, depending on the machine and UNIX implementation.

Ease of use

UNIX, as an operating system, is difficult to get to grips with. It would be unwise, therefore, for the novice desktop publisher to leap on the SoftQuad bandwagon unless UNIX expertise is readily available. Indeed, the attraction of this composition system must realistically be said to apply for existing UNIX users only. As yet, there is no true WYSIWYG facility other than the preview feature, nor is a WIMP-like user interface in place. We understand that moves are being made in that direction, but to date SoftQuad, though simple in comparison to troff in its virgin state, cannot be classified as easy.

Interleaf: a serious contender

Possibly the most serious contender in UNIX-based publishing systems is the Interleaf Corporation. Their product, Interleaf Workstation Publishing Software (WPS), is implemented on the IBM 6150 UNIX machine, in addition to DEC, Sun and Apollo configurations. Interleaf WPS offers the UNIX user a WIMPs and WYSIWYG environment, and is thus far less daunting than packages along the lines of SoftQuad. To date, it has been used mainly for technical and/or corporate publications. The reason for the former stems from the traditional role of UNIX in the field of CAD/CAM. Whereas DTP on the stand-alone micro has its roots in the text editing/wp environment, UNIX-based DTP tends to have evolved from existing graphics systems, and the emphasis, to a certain extent, lies in this direction.

Interleaf is a document-based composition system. The processing power of the current generation of supermicros makes them admirable stable companions for such packages. The speed with which overall document formatting occurs could not be equalled on a comparable PC-based composition system.

Icon-based user interface

Given that the desktop publisher has learnt to expect his WIMPs environment, Interleaf has provided a user-friendly interface that serves to provide this and, perhaps more significantly, to shield the user from the complexities of UNIX. In many respects, Interleaf WPS operates in much the same way as the single-user software outlined above. Hence the mouse supplements keyboard entry, pull-down menus are supported and a cut-and-paste facility allows text and graphics to be moved from one document to another.

Obviously, the same limitations are present as on an MS-DOS-based system, i.e. once the user interface is exited, one is confronted with the operating system in its raw (and not so friendly) form. The facility to cut and paste will not, therefore, apply overall to any and all software on the system. We have already established that in this facility the Macintosh is unique, and will not now labour the point.

Text editing

Interleaf offers some facilities normally associated with wordprocessing software, such as:

- Search and replace
- Automatic spelling check
- 'Goto' facility to avoid laborious scrolling

Text can be accepted in a variety of formats and from various wp environments, including DCA, Wang, Xerox 860 and WordStar. Indeed, Interleaf includes a communications program that allows data transfer from PCs operating under MS-DOS. Nroff (a less sophisticated relation of troff) files are also supported.

As with the majority of page make-up systems explored above, Interleaf WPS is not designed for text input, though editing at all levels is permitted.

Formatting

A 'stylesheet' or boilerplate facility allows the preformatting of documents, in terms of columns, justification, etc. The preformatting of typeface components, however, requires the use of a 'property sheet'.

Real-time automatic pagination and formatting occurs as text is fed into the document, or when edits and alterations are made. Widow and orphan controls can be specified.

Automatic hyphenation and justification is fully supported. Hyphenation is based on an algorithm plus an 86,000 word dictionary that is user-expandable. Line spacing can be controlled and specified in the property sheet.

Graphics and Interleaf support

Interleaf supports the 'frame' concept for the creation of graphics and their subsequent incorporation into the document. Three graphics types are available:

(1) Business graphics. Over 40 types of charts and graphs can be generated from data input directly by the user. The communications option also allows graphic files to be accepted from PC-based packages such as Lotus 1-2-3, VisiCalc and Multiplan. Data held in tabular form anywhere in the document can be transferred into chart format.

(2) Free form diagrams. Interleaf provides graphics primitives for the creation of rules, curved lines, boxes, circles and ellipses. Objects, once generated, can be sized numerically. This makes use of 'sets ratio' to ensure precision. Alignment, grouping, duplication, rotation and movement of objects are also supported. Interleaf's free form graphics editor is based closely on the 'draw' family of software, in providing the same basic functions as MacDraw, and GEM Draw. A 'graphics cabinet' acts as a library for images to be pasted into any document. A selection of basic shapes, such as stars, borders, arrows, etc., are provided with the software. Customised shapes can also be retained for subsequent use.

(3) CAD files. Drawings created under CAD systems can be accepted into Interleaf documents in the following formats: output (print) files in Calcomp 960, Calcomp 925 and HPGL. The latter may be edited using Interleaf graphics tools.

PDL support

When first announced, Interleaf WPS provided no support for any industry standard page description language, much to the annoyance of DTP advocates. The system did not, therefore, support true fonts, but was supplied with 'Modern' and 'Classic' versions of Helvetica and Times respectively. A 'language' known as PMP organises the downloading of fonts as required for each page.

DEC's implementation of Interleaf wisely offers PostScript support. IBM's RT version is also available with DDL and recently announced PostScript drivers. This will obviously improve the situation. A package offering the flexibility and document formatting facilities of Interleaf would have met with limited acceptance if unable to provide output quality as professional as that available on the low end.

Macintosh and the IBM PC

With the implementation of standard PDL drivers, the UNIX user is no longer faced with the choice of powerful but demanding SoftQuad, or easier yet less able Interleaf.

Supermicros provide storage

Interleaf uses a supermicro with a hard disk system, and processing speeds and storage capacities beyond those of most personal computers. The Interleaf software runs on the Sun workstation (Sun Micro System) with 2 megabytes of memory and a 42 megabyte hard disk system. This is the hardware that is often associated with CAD/CAM workstations, giving some indication of the quality that can potentially be provided with these UNIX-based systems.

Other benefits

As mentioned above, there are a number of other benefits, one of which comes into play when large documents have to be processed. Interleaf, running on a UNIX-based system, can repaginate long documents in seconds, whereas a personal computer might take minutes. The system can also be interfaced to typesetting machines such as the Monotype, Compugraphic, Autologic and Information International typesetters. The Interleaf system now provides professional-quality page layout capabilities.

Other contenders in the UNIX marketplace

Increasingly, it is the high-end software developers and hardware manufacturers who are subsuming desktop publishing into the office automation environment. This is all well and good for the corporate user, who provides the bulk of the business for companies such as Digital, Apollo, Sun and even IBM.

This has led to many of the more recent UNIX-based desktop publishing offerings being provided as part of a total office system. Altos, manufacturer of the most widely installed UNIX system in the UK, has announced the AOM DeskSet Publisher. Forming part of the Altos Officer Manager Suite, the system offers adequate typographical features for the corporate user though, as yet, no PDL support.

However, this tendency to view desktop publishing as part of the total office automation strategy may hinder its ultimate development along the path towards higher typographical standards and higher quality output. Is the corporate publisher, operating in a multi-user environment, to develop a complacent attitude towards composition standards, and merely subjugate desktop publishing to the level of enhanced document production within the office automation strategy? Should we therefore turn our attention back to the single-user PC, as the great white hope of the desktop publishing industry?

Chapter Six
Front-end Peripherals and Other Add-Ons

There are many elements in desktop publishing: personal computers, software, skills and peripherals. These peripherals are both back-end and front-end. The front-end peripherals are those that can be used to accept data into the system, whereas back-end peripherals are used to output copy. There have been a number of developments in both areas, all of which are designed to assist the desktop publisher. The most important front-end devices are the keyboard and the mouse. These are implicit in the process of entering data, and of manipulation, selection and all the requirements of day-to-day operation.

The most significant contribution to desktop publishing in terms of recently developed front-end devices is the graphic digitiser.

Graphic digitisers

A graphic digitiser converts an image into digitised information that a personal computer processes, stores, displays on the screen and prints on a printer. Once a display has been digitised and displayed on a computer screen as an image, it is then possible to use special graphics software to edit and enhance it. This can include scaling, cropping, editing, and adding and deleting sections, often working at pixel level. The image can then be exported into page layout software and placed in the text of the publication.

Image scaling
This process is more complicated than it sounds, because scaling images down to a size causes image distortion, sometimes rendering them unusable. However, with the advent of more sophisticated scanning software, the need for manual scaling (i.e. 'picking up' the corner of a graphic and moving it inwards or outwards in order to enlarge or reduce it) is less important. Enhanced scanning software

allows the scaling to be specified in terms of percentage increases or decreases, which avoids the possibility of distorted images.

The LaserWriter can enhance the enlargement/reduction facilities, since it offers a range of 15 per cent reduction to 100 per cent enlargement at 300 dpi. One may therefore have to use the output device to achieve acceptable hard copy of a scanned image, and then resort to manual cut-and-paste. As a means of achieving precision scaling at the required resolution, this can be tiresome.

In order to place an image in a publication, the precise area allocated for the graphic has to be established and the size of the scanned original calculated. Images can then be reduced or enlarged before they are placed in the composition software. Not all image scanners allow this precise scaling.

The success of solving problems such as image distortion depends on the functions provided by the digitising software and the graphics program. A standard function of even the most rudimentary digitisers enables the user to alter digitised images, changing their contrast, brightness and grey scale.

Editing scanned images

Once scanned in, images can be transferred into a freehand graphics package for editing. The reason that the lower resolution 'paint' packages are used rather than their higher resolution 'structured graphics' counterparts lies in their ability to 'blow up' sections of the image. This enables editing at pixel level, in order to smooth fuzzy lines, add or delete legends, or even make drastic changes. The problem of reduced resolution can be overcome because enhancements to scanning software enable the image, though edited at 72 dpi resolution, to be reinstated at 300 dpi. The quality is increased if images are scanned as large as possible (though one can only currently scan up to A4 on typical desktop publishing devices) and then reduced prior to incorporation into the document.

Scanners are of particular value when combining very detailed technical diagrams into reports and other publications. Line drawings always produce results superior to half-tones.

Several types of digitisers can be used with personal computers; all convert an image into binary information that the computer can process and store. One digitising method uses video cameras to capture an image on the computer. The video camera is connected to a digitiser and the camera is focused on the subject. Digitisers convert the signal from the camera into a stream of binary information and relay it to the computer where it is stored. The digitiser and the software distinguish various tones of grey in the video image and reproduce patterns of black and white dots on the screen. By combining or altering the patterns, different shades of grey that define the shape of the image are provided.

Video digitisers

The earliest digitisers available for desktop publishing were those dependent on a video camera to capture the image. The digitiser is connected to a black and white video camera at one end and to the personal computer serial port at the other. Once the camera and digitiser are set up, the digitising software is loaded, the lens is focused on the subject, and the digitiser builds up an image on the screen in anything from 0.1 to 5 seconds.

The precision and aesthetic 'look' of the digitised image will depend on several factors, including the standard and type of video lens provided – ideally, a 12.5 mm to 75 mm zoom. The camera and lighting must be set up for each object to be digitised. If line drawings are to be captured, the use of a lighted copystand will improve results.

The system allows adjustment to focus, contrast and brightness of the screen image, but requires judgment in designing the camera angle, or staging. This can only be done with training and practice, and a modicum of photographic know-how.

Results can differ enormously. We have used video digitisers to produce interesting 'half-tones' of physical objects (such as people!) which we could not have achieved with a scanner. On the whole, however, the primary use of digitisers in the DTP environment is to capture line drawings that are too complex/time-consuming to reproduce. In this area the video method leaves too much room for operator error and external influences such as lighting, to detract from quality results. One advantage of a video digitiser, however, is that the image is produced in a matter of seconds. Macintosh-based video digitisers include New Image Technology's Magic (MAcintosh Graphics Input Controller) and Microvision's MacViz desktop publishing. The latter, though more costly, offers a superior lens and is supplied complete with illuminated copystand.

Optical scanners

Optical scanners are a second type of digitiser used with PC-based desktop publishing systems. These scanners do not use a video camera but scan an optical device across a flat image, such as a photo or drawing, and digitise the information read from it.

Thunderware's Thunderscan

An optical digitiser in its most rudimentary form is Thunderscan – an optical scanner that can be used with a Macintosh computer. The scanner cartridge, a light-sensitive device, replaces the ribbon cartridge of Macintosh's ImageWriter printer. The photo or illustration to be digitised is inserted in the printer. When scanning, the scanner head reads back and forth across the image, gathering digitised information as the illustration advances through the printer. As it moves, it points a thin stream of light at the image, reads the lightness or darkness of many small spots, and converts the information into numeric (binary) values, which are stored in the computer's memory. The digitiser then analyses the binary information and converts it into the dot patterns that become the printed image.

After the optical reader has been inserted, the scanner is connected at the back of the printer and then to the Macintosh printer port. Half-tones and line drawings up to an A4-sized sheet can be captured. Thunderscan's software allows adjustment to the contrast and brightness of an image and also limited editing of the captured image, redrawing, copying, and cutting and pasting portions of the image. An image can be magnified up to 400 per cent, provided it is on the standard A4 page, or reduced to 25 per cent of its original size. The digitised image is saved as a MacPaint file for further editing and eventual transfer to the page composition program.

Additional video equipment is not needed – only an ImageWriter printer. The main drawbacks of Thunderscan are the slow scanning speed and the low resolution produced. Scanning can take up to 15 minutes as the scanning head moves back and forth across the image in tiny increments. The larger the image to be digitised, the longer the scanning takes. Moreover, if one is to output at 300 dpi or via typesetting equipment at 1200 or 2400 dpi, it must be possible to scan in at a comparable resolution.

Thunderscan is not recommended for desktop publishers who have a need for quality scanning equipment, since the amount of pixel editing required to smooth fuzzy edges is excessive. In addition, it requires an ImageWriter printer to operate the system.

Thunderscan's significance in desktop publishing

Because of its low price (sub-£300), Thunderscan is still considered to be a viable addition to the desktop publishing system. The initial cost economy, though, may be lost in terms of increased time, and frustration over poor results.

Thunderscan's importance lies in the fact that, as a front runner in

Inbuilt Fonts

The Dataproducts LZR - 2665 PostScript printer has thirteen inbuilt type fonts: These Fonts are available in a variety of sizes from 4 point to 127 point.

Times Roman
Times Bold
Times Italic
Times Bold Italic

Courier
Courier Oblique
Courier Bold
Courier Bold Oblique

Helvetica
Helvetica Oblique
Helvetica Bold
Helvetica Bold Oblique

Symbol/Math
Symbol/Math

Downloadable Fonts

Additional downloadable fonts are available from Adobe which give designers and typographers an even wider choice of type styles.

These fonts include:
Palatino
ITC Bookman
ITC Zapf
ITC Avant Garde
New Century Schoolbook
Optima
ITC Souvenir
ITC Lubalin
ITC Garamond
ITC American Typewriter
ITC Benguiat

Glypha
Trump
Melior
ITC Galliard
ITC New Baskerville
ITC Korinna
Goudy Old Style
Sonata
Century Old Style
ITC Franklin Gothic
ITC Cheltenham
Park Avenue
Bodoni
Letter Gothic
Prestige Elite
Orator

Inbuilt Font Styles

Plain

Italic

Bold

Bold Italic

Underline

Outline

Shadow

Plain
Italic
Bold
Bold Italic
Underline
Outline
Shadow

Fig. 6.1   Sample of output from Dataproducts' LzR 2665.

the pre-LaserWriter days, it established certain precedents. In generating market awareness as to the value of document scanners, it has led to the evolution of higher-level products. The state-of-the-art desktop publishing system would, without the scanner, be less flexible and hold less appeal. In simple terms, the more sophisticated products outlined below are the results of enhancements on a general theme.

Other types of digitisers

A third type of digitiser scans images using a mechanism similar to that found in a photocopier. A flat image, such as a photograph, is placed on the scanner and lit with a low frequency light. The image is reflected from a mirror and focused through a lens to a bank of electronic elements called charged coupled devices, or CCDs, that sense light and dark areas and convert them into binary data (ones and zeros). The digitised information is then sent to the computer as an image.

Microtek MS 300A/Abaton 300

One scanner that uses an array of CCDs is the Microtek MS 300A (a badged version of the Abaton 300), which works with both the IBM range and compatibles, and with the Macintosh. A page is inserted into the scanner, and rolls past the light-sensitive element during scanning. It can scan pages up to A4, with a scanning time of less than 20 seconds. However, this depends on how the graphic is constructed: half-tones will take longer to scan than line drawings, for example.

Versascan and Cscan, the software supplied with the Abaton, allow seven different modes of scanning suited for a mix of text, graphics and pictures, with multiple grey levels. Various viewing levels are supported as an aid to the editing function. The scanner is smaller than a typical dot matrix printer and can be conveniently placed on a desktop near the computer.

A sample image digitised by the MS 300A appears in Fig. 6.2. As the name implies, the MS 300A scans in at a resolution of 300 dpi – in keeping with the LaserWriter.

Another scanner of note is the Canon 1X-12. Originally sold exclusively as part of Canon's total DTP offering, it is now available as a stand-alone unit. Much more compact than the Microtek/Abaton, it offers the same resolution.

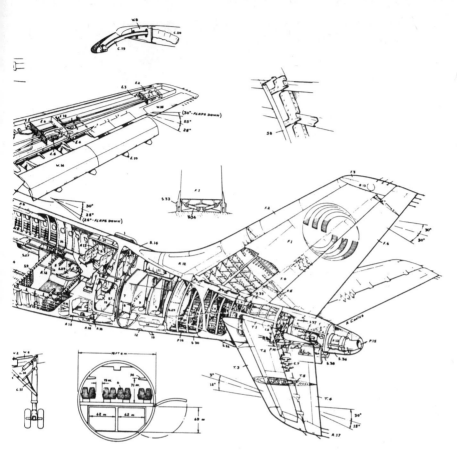

Fig. 6.2   Standard image produced using the MS 300A scanner.

Storage of scanned images

It should be noted that most scanned images (produced from scanners of the Abaton type) can be stored in compressed or non-compressed mode. Moreover, in order to accept and process a graphics image of A4 size more than 1 megabyte of RAM is required. While the Macintosh RAM can be upgraded from 1 to 4 megabytes, this is less easy on the IBM PC and compatibles since MS-DOS limits available address space to 640K bytes. Additional memory boards can overcome this limitation. An image can be 'uncompressed' for the purposes of editing and printing. Often it is not necessary to hold large images on the hard disk, and they can therefore be stored on a library of floppy disks.

The Macintosh's inbuilt Scrapbook proves to be a great benefit for

Fig. 6.3 Example of halftone produced using the MS 300A scanner.

holding reusable scanned images such as logos, standard symbols, etc., which are normally small and do not consume disk space. Images held in the Scrapbook rather than in separate files can be more readily pasted into documents.

In most cases, the quality of scanned half-tones is not acceptable for professional or even near-professional publications, although they do have a place in the desktop publishing environment. See Figure 6.3.

Scanning standards

As with many innovative products in the desktop publishing arena, standards for scanning equipment are emerging. First, it is recognised that scanning at resolutions less than 300 dpi is not acceptable for anything other than very rudimentary DTP. Secondly, the software provided should allow scanned images to be captured, stored and transferred in Tag ImageFile format (TIFF), the scanning equivalent of ASCII.

The current market leaders in the field of page make-up will accept TIFF format (PageMaker, Ventura Harvard Professional Publisher), hence to opt for a scanner that does not output in TIFF effectively locks the desktop publisher into one manufacturer. The adoption of TIFF will also allow the upgrade of scanning hardware/software while still reusing previously scanned images.

External scanning services

Scanners are excellent for producing graphics for desktop publications, and can be fun to use. If it is not possible to justify the purchase of a scanner, seek out an independent graphic professional who specialises in digital graphics. These people will often quote a price on a job-by-job basis to transform illustrations into final art.

Not many shops exist at the moment, but if one is available they can be a handy resource for the desktop publisher. It is possible to take a photograph to almost any local printer and have it screened and sized for a fee.

PC Scan

DEST – in the scanning market for many years – has produced a product, not only smaller and faster than many of its earlier models, but one that also doubles as an optical character reader (OCR).

PC Scan operates with IBM PCs and compatibles. It is compact, neat and very small; indeed, the entire unit sits between IBM PC monitor and system unit. To date, the OCR reads most standard monospaced typefaces, letter Gothic, Prestige Elite, Courier PICA, etc., only at 10 or 12 pitch. Some proportionally spaced fonts are also supported. Moreover, PC Scan is able to read typefaces produced by many of the most widely used dot matrix printers.

PC Scan's Text PAC software allows, it is claimed, the input of text at rates up to 30 times faster than the average typist can type. In certain cases, particularly when a previously manual system is being computerised and hence all documentation is typewritten, a product like PC Scan obviously proves invaluable.

These products are useful tools for the desktop publisher and, once standards have been defined and accepted, there will be a stream of useful developments.

Chapter Seven
Back-end Peripherals and Add-Ons

It is the back-end peripherals that provide the printed material that is read by the desktop publisher's customers. In the main, these peripherals are laser devices: page printers or typesetters, that serve to output the hard copy required for the printing process.

Laser printers

Until recently, laser printers were mainly used in universities and corporate institutions where high-volume printing was needed. High-capacity laser printers such as the Xerox 9700 or the IBM 66 700 are roughly the size of a household deepfreeze and range in price from £50,000 to £250,000. They are run by mainframe minicomputers and are usually located in computer centres surrounded by technicians and humming equipment that provide data processing services to a multi-terminal computer network.

Such laser printers are popular today in large organisations that can afford them, because they print hundreds of pages per hour over extended time periods and produce documents of the quality that professional and business standards require. Fortunately for desktop publishing, technology has brought laser printing into an affordable price range.

Laser printers, such as the Apple LaserWriter, Hewlett Packard LaserJet and ImageGen H/300, are available today at prices ranging from £2000 to £7000.

These printers produce documents of a resolution many dots per inch above the dot matrix and letter-quality printers commonly used with personal computers. Dot matrix printers produce characters composed of many small dots printed closely together – the more, the closer and the smaller the dots, the finer the look of the character they compose. The Apple ImageWriter, for example, prints characters at a resolution of about 80 dpi. Laser printers such as the LaserJet Plus and the LaserWriter, however, print more clearly defined characters at a resolution of up to 300 dpi. Resolutions of 1000 to 25,000 dpi are commonly produced by professional typesetting equipment; hence the laser printer-type fonts with a resolution of 300 dpi will resemble the same typesetting font in size and shape, but differ considerably in resolution.

Laser printers output text using a mixture of font types, sizes and styles, and they are able, to a greater or lesser extent, to integrate text and graphics on a page. No letter-quality or dot matrix printer can mix fonts and print graphics so successfully. Changing fonts with the letter-quality printer usually requires that you stop the printer and replace a print element, such as a daisywheel or another element holding a different font size or style. Letter-quality printers are often limited to font sizes ranging from 17 to 10 pixels wide and 9 to 12 points high. Some dot matrix printers mix fonts and print characters at various sizes. With laser printers such as the LaserWriter, however, you can print characters of point sizes from 3 up to 255, the range being limited only by the software. Some laser printers produce pages with a mixture of typeface sizes and styles in one continuous printing, without the need to stop and change print control elements.

Laser printers are much faster than most letter-quality printers used with personal computers today. Print speeds with letter-quality printers are 80 to 90 characters per second. Laser printers' speeds vary depending on the amount of text and graphics on the page. With the LaserWriter, for example, setting up a complex image for printing can take several minutes. However, laser printers can obtain printing speeds of 325 characters per second, or roughly 8 to 10 pages per minute, when printing the same page repeatedly. Moreover, such speeds are obtained at the noise level of a quiet conversation – approximately 55 decibels – which is remarkably quiet compared to the racket commonly produced by dot matrix and letter-quality printers. The latest laser printers fit on a desk, leaving sufficient room for PC, scanner, keyboard and mouse.

Combined text and graphics

The ability to output combined text and graphics at high resolution has made desktop publishing feasible by enabling the production of clean, camera-ready copy. Moreover, copy that makes use of industry standard typefaces can be output directly to a professional typesetting device, without degrading the precision of layout.

Print engine and image processor

Laser printers are basically composed of two elements: a laser-actuated marking engine, called the print engine, and an image processing system. The LaserWriter, LaserJet, and ImageGen 8/300 all share the same Canon LBP-CX print engine.

A laser printer engine produces images using a hair-fine beam of laser light (see Fig. 7.1). The laser light is directed into a rapidly

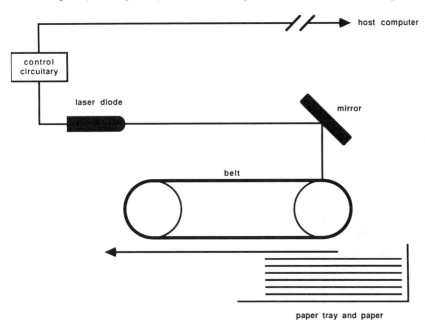

Fig. 7.1 How a laser printer works.

revolving hexagonal mirror that scans the light in a fine line across a large photosensitive drum. According to image data relayed from the image processor, the laser beam pulses on and off; each pulse of laser light charges a small spot on the rotating drum. As the drum rotates, the electronically charged spot on the drum attracts fine toner powder from a toner cartridge. The drum comes in contact with the paper and transfers the toner to it, using a combination of heat and pressure. The many dots fuse to produce a crisp, clear image of text and graphics. The Canon LBP-CX print engine produces 90,000 dots per square inch (300 dpi × 300 dpi), to produce well defined characters.

Different printers using the same engine

Although many laser printers from different manufacturers use the same print engine, printing capabilities differ because the image processing systems differ. This system is run by a powerful computer built into the printer. The Apple LaserWriter, for example, contains a high-speed 68000 processor and 2 megabyte of memory. It has more processing power memory than many personal computers. The Hewlett Packard LaserJet uses the same microprocessor, but only has 128K of memory within the machine. A great deal of memory is required to hold an image composed of so many small dots and produce it in a variety of styles and sizes. Differences in memory size and in font and processing information stored in a printers' memory greatly affect the printers' capabilities.

Desktop laser-printing – early developments

The Hewlett Packard LaserJet, introduced in September 1984, was acclaimed as the first low-cost printer that allowed personal computer users laser performance at an affordable price. Since then the flood gates have opened, leading to a plethora of products, based initially on the Canon LBP-CX print engine, and latterly on the Ricoh 4080 which allows heavier-duty usage. While the earlier products provided nothing in the way of support for page description languages, and were primarily aimed at the wordprocessing market, today we are witnessing a wealth of new laser printing devices, offering improved speeds, paper size options, resilience and design, that are aimed at the desktop publishing market.

To shed some light on the growing range of available printers, let us look at four laser printers appropriate to desktop publishing and examine their principal capabilities. Of course, there are many more sophisticated laser printers in higher price ranges, but if you acquaint yourself with the following laser printers you will be on your way to a firm understanding of available laser technology.

The Apple LaserWriter

The Apple LaserWriter is an excellent printer for desktop publishing, and can be said to have made desktop publishing a reality. Its image processing system and large memory (2 megabyte of RAM and ROM combined) enable it to print full pages of text and graphics at 300 dpi resolution.

Page size is limited by the hardware constraints of the Canon LPB-CX engine, which cannot print true A4: an area of approximately 7 mm is cut off every side of the page. Page set-up instructions allow the user to specify A4 (or its close approximation), US legal, and B5. One can opt to print in either landscape (wide) or portrait (tall) modes. Scaling can be specified precisely, merely by keying in a percentage for enlargement or reduction.

When using the LaserWriter with the Macintosh, the page set-up screen is constant regardless of which software is running (i.e. desktop publishing, wordprocessing, spreadsheet, etc.) and hence allows the same range of facilities. (See Fig. 7.2 for an illustration of LaserWriter page set-up.)

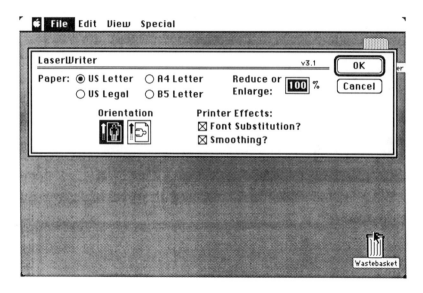

Fig. 7.2 LaserWriter page set-up.

The reason for this consistent approach to laser printing is that the laser printer driver resides in the Macintosh operating system, and as such is not application package specific. By extension, therefore, all Macintosh software can be printed out at 300 dpi, and most packages can access industry standard fonts resident in the LaserWriter.

One notable exception to this is MacPaint – Apple's freehand graphics software. Given that MacPaint was designed with the dot matrix ImageWriter in mind, it can only output at 72 dpi. Obviously, this is inadequate for the desktop publisher, who is turning to alternative products such as FullPaint and SuperPaint, both of which output at the acceptable 300 dpi.

The laser printer can mix text and graphics on the page. For example, with the Macintosh it is possible to use page layout software to format page and images on the screen and then print fully composed pages on the laser printer. With the traditional page layout methods, the text is composed on a typesetting machine. The composed text is then prelined on paste-up boards, leaving spaces for graphics. The graphics are then pasted into place. The LaserWriter's ability to print a full page of graphics and text means that the paste-up step is skipped. Apple's LaserWriter is one of the first laser printers to use industry standard typefaces identical in every respect to that used by professional typesetting machines.

The LaserWriter and LaserWriter Plus

Two versions of the Apple laser printer are now available: the LaserWriter and the LaserWriter Plus. In keeping with Apple's commitment to upgradability, the former can be modified to Plus specification. This operation involves a logic board change, and is a simple task (though not one to be performed by the user).

The differences between the two models lie in speed; the standard LaserWriter outputs at up to eight pages a minute if repeating the same page, whereas the Plus offers a top speed of ten pages a minute – as indeed do most of its rivals. The second difference lies in the number of ROM-based fonts supplied with the printer.

Fonts

The following ROM-based font families are available on the Laser-Writer Plus as additions to those supplied with the basic model: Helvetica Narrow, Avant Garde, Palatino, Bookman, Zapf Chancery, New Century School Book, Dingbats.

Given that there are obvious limits to the number of type families that can reasonably reside in the LaserWriter's 0.5 megabyte of ROM, Apple selected from the Adobe library of Allied and ITC fonts those type families that were considered to offer widest appeal to the desktop publisher. These may not always prove adequate for the professional printer who, having adopted and implemented a house style, wishes to retain continuity by adhering to the selected typeface. Univers, for example, is often cited as a font that PR companies, advertising agencies – indeed, the 'media' industry in general – would like to see implemented. Moreover, it must not be forgotten that the UK publishing industry does not precisely mirror its US counterpart. US companies are widely accepted to be more tolerant of low-quality resolution, and hence to use laser-written output in situations where it would be greeted with horror by the self-respecting UK production manager. Many of the type families supplied with the LaserWriter may therefore have limited appeal.

This problem is overcome through the use of downloadable fonts. These are supplied and licensed by Adobe, as are the resident type families, and are disk based. Fonts are loaded through the Macintosh and remain in the printer until it is switched off and to all intents and purposes the process is transparent to the user. The additional font merely appears as another option on the pull-down menu. Download-able fonts contain the entire type family, i.e. roman, italic, bold, and all other versions of the font supported by the LaserWriter. Given that a family will typically use about 40K of RAM, one is limited to downloading only two or three simultaneously. However, for most users this is more than adequate.

The choice of available fonts is increasing rapidly. The LaserWriter comes with three typeface families stored in ROM: Helvetica, Times and Courier. Times and Helvetica are commonly used in commercial typesetting of standard publications. Times is a 'serif' font, of the type generally used for the bulk of text since it is considered easier to read. Helvetica is a 'sans serif' font and is more widely used for headings to which the uncluttered, clear appearance lends itself. Courier is similar to typefaces found on typewriters and daisywheel printers.

All available fonts support the full European character set: graves, cedillas, umlauts, etc. Furthermore, the Macintosh allows any feature – for example, an acute accent – to be appended to any character, not just those characters that conform to typical combinations.

Each font family can be printed in four styles from a choice of roman, italic (or oblique), bold roman and bold italic (or oblique). Samples of LaserWriter font styles are given in Fig. 7.3. These typefaces can also be printed underlined, shadowed or outlined, or in any combination of the above.

The Apple Macintosh directs the LaserWriters' printing using a page description programming language called PostScript. Any software that is supplied with PostScript language drivers can use the LaserWriter's many typefaces during printing.

	Times
Roman	In essence WP is the manipulation and arrangement of words. Unlike using a
	typewriter, the words do not go directly onto paper: they appear on a screen
Bold	**which becomes the medium for alterations and edits. Only when**
	the entire document is correct is it commited to paper. In this
Italic	*way a great deal of effort is saved, and the operator is free to work at the full*
	typing speed, since any errors can be put right later.
Bold/Italic	***The total saving in time can be quite dramatic, and the final***
	printed output can be free from the ubiquitous typex and manual
	Helvetica
Roman	edits that once had to be endured.
	Through the use of wordprocessing, moreover, standard documents
Bold	**can be stored for subsequent editing and re-use, cutting**
	down on operator time at every re-draft.
Italic	*The Development of Wordprocessing*
	The original generation of wordprocessors used special purpose
Bold/Italic	***hardware, dedicated to wordprocessing. However, the***
	various components of the system, screen, keyboard,

Fig. 7.3 Sample of font styles.

Diablo emulation

The LaserWriter can also emulate a Diablo 630 printer, and other computers can use it as if they were using the Diablo 630. Software that does not output PostScript code can send information to the printer if it has a Diablo 630 print driver. When it is emulating a Diablo 630 printer, however, the laser printer works like the Diablo letter-quality printer and special features, such as its many typefaces, cannot be used.

Computers such as the IBM PC and compatibles can take full advantage of the LaserWriter's printing capacities when they run software that transmits data in a PostScript format. The IBM PC can be used with Microsoft Word, Samna and other wordprocessing software as well as graphic programs such as GEM Draw and Paint and, of course, page layout software.

PostScript was created specially for high-resolution laser printers. The LaserWriter's PostScript interpreter converts simple commands from an external computer, such as a Macintosh, into text and images produced by the laser printer. In the PostScript language, each text character is defined by the program's mathematical formulas, or outlines. Using these outlines, the PostScript interpreter directs the printer to build up a bit map of the page in RAM. PostScript also directs the graphic capabilities of the printer; in fact, it treats both text and graphics as images.

PostScript

Using PostScript to run the LaserWriter brings another outstanding benefit: PostScript is one of the first page description languages that has gained acceptance among typesetter manufacturers.

Postscript supports professional typesetting equipment, such as Linotype's Linotron 100 and 300 series. Macintosh owners can hook up with a professional typesetter to create a camera-ready bromide of a document at a resolution of up to 2500 dpi. A Macintosh and a LaserWriter can be used to produce documents at a resolution of 300 dpi for draft purposes. The same document can then be sent to a phototypesetter for high-quality output. Given PostScript's use of industry standard fonts, one can be confident that the output from the LaserWriter will be identical to the Linotron output in all layout respects. The desirability of using industry standard 'Licensed' fonts as opposed to 'bastardised' versions – i.e. close approximations that are implemented, generally, to save on the copyright costs – are obvious.

The LaserWriter can print up to eight pages per minute, but this maximum rate is obtained only when repeating printing a page stored in memory. A single page that includes multiple font changes, obliquing, underlining and other enhancements can take several minutes to be transmitted and printed by a LaserWriter.

The LaserWriter is designed to print about 3000 pages per month. Moreover, it requires mandatory servicing at 50,000 page intervals. Do not expect to use the LaserWriter as a printing press to print multiple issues of a publication numbering hundreds. First, it would be a very expensive way of producing copies. Second, the printing paper tray does not hold more than 100 sheets at a time, and the output tray holds only 50 sheets at a time. This means that an operator must be present to refill and empty page trays when printing large numbers of pages.

Like desktop copiers, the LaserWriter uses dry toner cartridges for printing. A single cartridge costs roughly £100 and will last for approximately 3000 printed pages, depending on the amount of text and graphics per page. It is generally reckoned that the cost of printing one A4 sheet is about 3p – comparable to photocopying costs.

AppleTalk – peripheral sharing network

The LaserWriter supports the Apple personal network system. AppleTalk is a low-cost network, orientated primarily towards peripheral sharing. It can theoretically support up to 32 devices, including Macintoshes, LaserWriters and Imagewriter IIs (with the addition of an internal AppleTalk card), in addition to IBM PCs and compatibles. The latter can be connected via a special AppleTalk interface card that allows coexistence with the Macintosh, and by extension the use of the LaserWriter as a shared resource. The recent entry of IBM DTP software into the arena has created a demand for precisely the solution that the AppleTalk card provides. We anticipate a wealth of similar products in the very near future.

The LaserWriter can be linked serially to the IBM PC and, given software with PostScript drivers, will allow the user access to all its benefits. Moreover, the device can be shared by a number of PCs networked with any of the standard LAN offerings (Novell Torus, etc.)

Realistically, it is not recommended that 31 Macintoshes, for example, share one LaserWriter. While AppleTalk can cover significant distances (1000 feet, with the option for bridging two networks together and thus increasing the distance considerably), there is currently no spooling facility supplied as standard. What this means, in effect, is that whichever user excecutes the print command first will be able to print; all others who attempt to do so will be given a message advising them that user X is printing and offering the option to cancel the print command. Obviously, the implications for users working in remote offices are quite laborious. Apart from ringing a colleague and asking how long the print run in progress will take, one can only keep excecuting the print command until the LaserWriter is free.

Thankfully, print spoolers can be obtained as add-ons to the system, which serve to overcome this problem. The prospective desktop publisher should carefully assess the anticipated print volumes before deciding on the system. Additionally, Apple has recently announced its own laserspooler which will shortly be available.

Hewlett Packard's LaserJet and LaserJet Plus

Despite their inherent unsuitability for the serious desktop publisher, the Hewlett Packard LaserJet and LaserJet Plus warrant inclusion in this guide for the simple reason that they made laser printing affordable and acceptable at the PC level. Designed around the same Canon print engine as the Apple LaserWriter, they print at the same speeds, with the same low decibel level, as their Apple counterpart.

The primary differences between Hewlett-Packard and Apple products lies in the processing power available, and in the lack of any page description language. Hence the LaserJet provides a mere 128K of combined RAM and ROM, and the LaserJet Plus 512K. Effectively, what this means to the user is that typefaces cannot reside in the printer: they are supplied as firmware on font cartridges and must be plugged into the printer as and when required.

Each font cartridge includes not a type family but various limited style and size options. One cartridge might hold, for example: Times roman 12 and 10 point, Times oblique 12, Courier 10 bold. Production of a document requiring several font size and style changes could necessitate numerous cartridge changes. Not only does this slow down the print processes, but it is cumbersome and decidedly unfriendly! Font sizes are limited, as are the choices available.

The restricted memory of the Hewlett Packard laser printers inhibits their value as graphics printers, since only a small portion of the page can be taken up with images. The LaserJet has found a definite niche as de facto leader in the PC-based wp arena. At less than £2000 for the basic model, its appeal against traditional daisywheel printers is significant. Moreover, it has met with some limited success as the output device for Clue, a page layout system running on the HP Vectra and IBM PC.

Hewlett Packard adopts DDL

What is significant for the purposes of this overview is Hewlett Packard's decision to adopt ImageGen's DDL (document description language) for its new generation of laser printers. The advantages of DDL against PostScript have been discussed above. Suffice it to say that the new laser printer will no doubt be greeted with a chorus of cheers by existing PC users, who are perhaps reluctant to adopt an Apple product (which continues, unfairly, to carry a non-industry-standard stigma within the 'true blue' IBM houses), and may already be using the original LaserJet for its wp function. Hewlett Packard wisely intends to provide an upgrade path for existing LaserJet users. This will involve swapping the logic board, and adding a RIP (raster image processor).

The majority of page layout software packages currently available on the IBM PC are rapidly developing DDL drivers (if they have not already done so) to take advantage of Hewlett-Packard's proposed products. In support of this move, ImageGen have announced a DDL controller in the form of a PC expansion card. This will allow PC users software independence, i.e. the ability to drive the printer regardless of whether DDL drivers are supplied with the software package in use. Once again, the industry appears to be following Apple's lead in allowing the user greater freedom in the choice of software without inhibiting output quality. The ImageGen DDL PC card also functions as a network print server/printer controller.

Dataproducts' LZR 2665

If today's desktop publisher were to devise a 'wish list' of attributes it would be desirable to see incorporated in a low cost system, doubtless A3 printing would appear high on the agenda. Yet A3 printing is available, and has been for some time. Agreed, costs are not in line with the sub-£10,000 mark desktop publishing purchasers are learning to expect, but by comparison with costs for professional typesetting equipment, and when viewed historically, the A3 laser is certainly more affordable than ever before.

A3 printing

Dataproducts was the first to launch a 'low-cost' A3 laser device, which not only adhered to the accepted standard of 300 dpi but offered full PostScript support. The Dataproducts LZR 2665 supports AppleTalk, in addition to offering parallel, RS232 and RS422 interfaces. Thirteen resident font families are supplied; others can be downloaded using precisely the same operation as is performed with the LaserWriter. While considerably more bulky than the LaserWriter or, indeed, the LaserJet, the LZR 2665 is designed for heavier-duty use and is able, once the image has been recreated in PostScript, to output at up to 26 pages per minute.

Whereas the strength of the LaserWriter lies in its ability to create camera-ready copy and artwork for subsequent printing on other equipment, the Dataproducts device has the ability to perform significant print runs. The printer's appeal and, indeed, success has been proportionately greater in the US than in the UK. This reinforces the view that the American market is less concerned about output quality and more likely to use an LZR 2665 to perform the entire task, through typesetting and printing, rather than turning to professional typesetting equipment in order to achieve increased resolution, and to professional printers for quantity runs. The Dataproducts laser printer has its place, given the A3 option and increased throughput speeds. The LZR 2665 A3 costs approximately £14,000. (See Fig. 6.1 on page 79 for sample output.)

The importance of page description languages (PDL)

Any discussion of desktop publishing would be incomplete without drawing the desktop publisher's attention to the benefits of page description languages (PDL). The majority of successful page layout software packages support a PDL (and those that do not have very little appeal), but laser manufacturers such as Hewlett Packard are in the process of developing a laser device offering a resident PDL.

The demarcation between PostScript (or PDL in general) laser printers and those without a page description language should be understood. This is absolutely fundamental, since any system without a PDL will have:

- Severe font limitations
- Difficulty accessing industry standard fonts
- Less flexibility in terms of output devices

While we have provided an overview of those printers that are establishing standards and proving currently to be de facto market leaders, there are others besides. Just as desktop publishing software is classified according to 'fitness for purpose', so we find that the same can be said of laser output devices – those suitable for sophisticated DTP and those geared to the wp function. Typically, a laser device of the latter type will offer no PDL and hence no RIP, since images will be built up in a different way. By extension, CRC cannot be output directly to any professional typesetting device which offers PDL support.

Limited appeal of non-PDL printers
Output device dependence reigns, with all the constraints that go with it. Fonts are in general 'bastardised' close approximations, font size is limited to 36 point, and full page graphics are not supported. Examples of laser printers of this type are many. Until such time as the manufacturers follow Apple's lead, as Hewlett Packard has done, their appeal to the desktop publisher is limited. Unfortunately, all too often the prospective buyer understands only that he must have 300 dpi resolution, and on that basis alone selects a printer that he will soon outgrow.

Thankfully, we are seeing considerable developments in laser devices which do offer PDL support. In the main, these are printers specifically developed with the desktop publishing market in mind, rather than upgraded wordprocessing output devices.

Print engines

Ricoh (previously of daisywheel fame) has recently developed the 4080 print engine which offers far greater resilience than the Canon. While monthly throughput using the Canon engine was reckoned to be 3000 pages (if the machine were to sustain a three-year life), the Ricoh is considered to allow 5000 pages per month over the same period. Sharp has also developed a print engine that is geared to greater resilience, not only to provide for a longer or more productive life, but also to cut down on maintenance charges by extending the period between overhauls.

Xerox is also offering a print engine that has been adopted by both QMS and ImageGen, though the latter continues to use the Canon for low-end devices. ImageGen printers support the ImPRESS PDL, while QMS has taken the safe route and opted for PostScript.

PostScript compatibility becomes reality

Apple recently announced UK distribution of Laser Connection's PS-Jet, a product that adds PostScript capabilities to Canon-based laser printers. The unit replaces the top cover assembly and is apparently user installable. It enables the upgraded printer to become fully LaserWriter compatible, and includes true Times, Helvetica, Symbol and Courier typefaces. Any PostScript software, either MS-DOS or Macintosh-based, can benefit from this enhancement. This move by Apple serves to reinforce their credibility as leaders in laser printing standards under both popular operating environments.

Xerox 4045

Lastly, the Xerox 4045, as supplied with Xerox's Documenter desktop publishing system, is worthy of mention since it is the only laser printer that doubles as a photocopier. (Well, what else should we expect from Xerox?) A reader resides on top of the unit, through which the original copy is run. In offering this option, Xerox cut down the use of the print engine in addition to freeing the printer when a multiple copy run is required. With a standard resolution of 300 dpi, the 4045 uses a combination of 'Bitstream' font cartridges and the InterPress PDL to build up pages.

Third-generation laser printers

Given the apparent need within the computer industry to categorise everything in terms of generations, it may shed light on past and future developments of PC-based laser devices to follow this example. The first generation encompasses the LaserJet lookalikes: 300 dpi printers offering limited font flexibility and limited graphics output, in short, the daisywheel replacements.

The second generation covers those printers also operating at 300 dpi but offering page description language support, expanded memory to allow for full page graphics printing and, ideally, access to industry standard typefaces.

The third generation will reflect the growing trend towards increased resilience, allowing more use of the device for larger print runs. In addition, it seems likely that we will witness a move away from the Motorola 68000 microprocessor adopted by both Apple and Datapro-ducts. The latter recently set the trend by moving to National Semiconductor's 32000 family in their LZR 2630. The NS 32000 provides more powerful bit manipulation capabilities for graphics output, faster processing and hence less waiting around while PostScript, or whichever PDL is in use, recreates the page for printing.

Colour laser printing

Colour laser printing, thought by pundits to be the next major development, is in reality far beyond the reach of desktop publishers. While the technology exists, and is in use, it is too expensive for the broad PC market. Indeed, until such time as the more sophisticated desktop publishing systems are able to perform colour separation, the average user will no doubt remain content with monochrome. Coloured toner cartridges are available for laser printers using the standard print engines, hence multiple pass printing could achieve at least limited and rudimentary spot colour output.

Increased resolution – the most important future development

The most dramatic change to emerge in the third generation laser printer is the increase in resolution. Canon and Ricoh already have print engines capable of 400 dpi and 600 dpi output. Undoubtedly, the existing, quite distinct line of demarcation between professional typesetting using devices such as the Linotype Linotronic 100 and 300, and desktop publishing will become increasingly nebulous, and perhaps arbitrary. However, the nature of the toner particles is currently such that extremely high resolutions are physically impossible to achieve.

The big screen

Despite its good resolution, the Macintosh's 9 inch screen has been a cause of considerable criticism – especially among those who have not even used it, but assume it will be difficult to work on for long periods. Yet one of the Macintosh's strengths is its small footprint (9 inches × 9 inches). The apparent dilemma has been overcome by the availability of add-on big screens which can simply be disconnected when not in use.

The success of desktop publishing has developed a demand for larger screens, in particular screens of true A4 size, which would help the page layout process.

Xerox Documenter sets the standard

Competition from Xerox's Documenter, which is supplied with either a 19 inch or a 15 inch monochrome paper white display, has led to Apple's recent announcement that its new open architecture Macintosh II will incorporate a large 12 inch screen, and will offer a variety of screen options. In the meantime, Macintosh users must content themselves with third-party add-on products, involving extra expense and rendering the built-in screen redundant.

Macintosh's big screens

The first big screen available for the Macintosh was the MegaScreen a 19 inch paper white display allowing for a resolution of up to 1024 × 1024 pixels (see Fig. 7.4). Costing around £2500, including graphics display card, the MegaScreen is certainly overpriced; but it was until relatively recently the only option available, and has hence capitalised on a monopolistic state of affairs. Sadly, not all Macintosh software is supported; hence MacPaint, for example, employs only a portion of the screen and offers no benefit whatsoever to the user. This, however, is not a reflection on the screen, but is a constraint found in some of the earlier Macintosh software.

Fig. 7.4 Photograph of MegaScreen and Macintosh Plus.

It is essential, therefore, in considering the purchase of a large screen, that the software to be used takes full advantage of the additional size. We found the MegaScreen ideal when using PageMaker and other desktop publishing software.

Moreover, it may be a consideration that the MegaScreen conforms to Trade Union regulations and stipulations regarding display size, which to date have effectively knocked the Macintosh out of the running in cases where union approval is mandatory.

Radius A4 screen

The Radius screen is true A4 size and, priced at £2000, offers a practical aid to the dedicated desktop publisher user. As with the MegaScreen, not all Macintosh software can benefit from the larger display area. PageMaker, Ready Set Go 3 and the majority of page make-up software will, however, make full use of the Radius screen.

A4 screens for the IBM PC and compatibles

The open architecture of the IBM PC lends itself to the addition of specialist screens. Hence the choices facing the IBM desktop publisher are far wider than those available to the Macintosh fraternity.

Micro Display Systems' Genius Full Page Display offers a resolution of 1008 × 736, or 100 dpi, an improvement over the resolution of

IBM's Enhanced Graphics Adaptor. The screen area measures 10 inches × 8 inches and displays 66 lines. The Genius supports the majority of DOS-based DTP, graphics and wp software. Priced at around £1800, the monitor is supplied with its own VHR display adaptor which is used in place of an EGA or Hercules card.

Wyse have produced a low-cost, high-resolution screen with the desktop publisher in mind. The Wyse 700 provides a resolution of 1280 × 800 when fitted with its own graphics adaptor. Despite being produced with a standard 15 inch display area, the high resolution and low price (£900 including graphics board) makes the Wyse an attractive proposition.

It has become apparent that future developments in the desktop publishing arena will take into account the desktop publisher's insistence on the large/high-resolution screen. Remember that the higher the screen resolution, the more readily you will really see what you are getting – and the sooner we can get away from WYSI(almost)WYG, the better!

Chapter Eight
The Difference Between Enhanced WP and Desktop Publishing

As manufacturers and software developers, desperate to jump on the desktop publishing bandwagon (in case the so-called revolution is quelled overnight), rush out their product offerings, the tendency is to take the shortest route to the desired end. It is expedient, or so they think, to beef up a wordprocessing package, add a facility for column support, and provide some links with graphics software. The moment of triumph arrives, of course, when they develop a page preview facility and immediately lay claim to the WYSIWYG environment – the goal of all desktop publishing software. Despite the Heath Robinson approach, success is guaranteed. Or is it?

The demarcation between true page composition systems and enhanced wordprocessors is currently quite clear to those who have used desktop publishing in earnest. We have attempted to define desktop publishing as we understand it, and it is on this understanding that we now examine below enhanced wordprocessing and its limitations for the desktop publisher. We also examine the potential convergence of the two technologies and its implications.

Wordprocessing – the first text editor

The concept of wordprocessing is simple; it is also a practice so common that we tend to adopt a blasé attitude to the benefits of this remarkable innovation, and wonder how we ever lived without it!

In essence, wordprocessing is the manipulation and arrangement of words. Unlike using a typewriter, the words do not go directly on to paper: they appear on a screen which becomes the medium for alterations and edits. Only when the entire document is correct is it committed to paper. In this way, a great deal of effort is saved and the operator is free to work at full typing speed, since any errors can be put right later.

The total saving in time can be quite dramatic, and the final printed output can be free from the unsightly manual edits that once had to be endured. Through the use of wordprocessing, moreover, standard documents can be stored for subsequent editing and reuse, cutting down on operator time at every redraft.

The development of wordprocessing

The original generation of wordprocessors used special purpose hardware, dedicated to wordprocessing. However, the various components of the system – screen, keyboard, disks, and so on – are the same in principle as those of the personal computer.

Today, there is no reason to use such a specialised machine in preference to the much more flexible PC. Since the early days of the microcomputer, wordprocessing packages have been available. These were once regarded as poor relations of the dedicated wordprocessor, with its specially configured keys that left little room for operator error or forgotten key strokes. By comparison, WordStar, as originally implemented on CP/M machines, was far from user-friendly.

Today's wordprocessing packages are extremely powerful, and generally emulate dedicated wordprocessing systems very closely. Indeed, they improve upon the latter, because of the facility of linking to other PC software: databases, spreadsheets, name and address lists and, more recently, to desktop publishing.

Wordprocessing today does not merely speed up the physical process of typing – it makes the whole task of document creation more rapid, efficient and effective. For this reason, organisations are normally far better advised to select equipment such as the PC, which offers the ability to process words and data, keep records or appointments, enable electronic communication – in short, to provide general personal computing. We should hence regard wordprocessing not as a piece of hardware but as a software option that can be run on every home and business computer.

Basic wordprocessing functions

All the widely accepted wordprocessing packages today are expected to offer certain basic functions. Making the statement, however, is easier than arriving at a list of precisely what those functions are. As a starting point, we have taken the features included in the current version of WordStar (the all-time de facto leader in PC wordprocessing software), which may be considered as a yardstick for comparison purposes.

Editing options

Many of the functions of a wordprocessor relate not to the initial input of text, which is relatively straightforward, but to editing and formatting text which already exists. Generally speaking, you have a choice of insert mode and overtype mode, which act on a 'toggle' basis, i.e. each mode can be switched on or off. In overtype mode, what is typed overwrites what was there before. In insert mode, the new text pushes the existing text to the right to make room. At this stage, WordStar requires the user to reformat the paragraph; in most current packages, reformatting is performed automatically.

Cursor movement

Cursor control allows movement around the text by line, character, screen or page. Scrolling through the text can be made more rapid by specifying begining or end of document. More recent wp software generally supports a 'goto' function, allowing the user to select the required page.

Search and replace

Specific words or character strings can be located in the document using the 'search' command. Once found, global or individual replacement can be specified. This is obviously of great value in cases such as standard letters or contracts where one merely wants to change a name or a date throughout the document.

Text movement

Using WordStar, text can be moved in blocks that require 'marking' through the use of control characters. Hence the reasonably logical command 'control KB' signifies the beginning of a block, and the less meaningful 'control KK' marks the end. One can thereafter specify whether the block is to be copied or moved, and mark the new position accordingly. The command for the latter is 'control KV'.

Text attributes

Depending on the printer in use, the attributes of the text can be defined – for instance, underline, bold, etc. Given a non-WYSIWYG environment, certain techniques are used to signify that certain blocks of text will be output in a specific style. Hence that portion of text may be displayed in reverse video mode.

Dot commands

WordStar allows the page length to be defined at the beginning of the document through the use of 'dot commands', not unlike the type of instructions that would be embedded in a standard non-WYSIWYG page composition program. Dot commands, (so called because each instruction is preceded by a dot) are effectively a message to the output device that the text is for reference only and must not be printed. Page breaks can be inserted at any point throughout the document, but this must be done manually. There is no automatic control over widows and orphans.

Other dot commands control top and bottom margins, headers, footers, page numbering, etc. – not particularly friendly, but highly effective (if the user can remember them all!).

Other features
Text can be justified, centred, or aligned left or right. Line spacing can be specified from 1 to 9 in one-line increments. Unlimited tabs can be placed throughout the document. Paragraph indents can be specified.

WordStar also offers a very rudimentary columnar facility, which often defeats the average user (present authors included!), and allows only one column per page.

Onscreen help
WordStar offers much-needed onscreen help, at various levels. The competent user is therefore presented with a blank screen, while the novice must contend with over a third of the available display being taken up with menus and options.

This very brief overview does not cover WordStar's full range of features. Indeed, despite disparaging asides, WordStar is a very powerful piece of software, as is borne out by the fact that it is still in use almost 10 years after it was first developed. What we intended to reveal was the functionality of the typical wordprocessing package, in order that an explanation of the new generation of 'enhanced wp' programs could be put in context.

Enhanced wordprocessing packages

There is a fairly clear line of demarcation between those wp packages that offer enhancements as a result of the need to compete with dedicated wordprocessing systems such as Wang, IBM's DisplayWriter and Digital's DECMate, and those that have done so in an attempt to penetrate the desktop publishing market. In some cases, there has been a logical development from one to the other; however, what is pertinent for the purpose of this discussion is to examine the latter, and their limitations for desktop publishing.

Modified vs. generic packages

If we take a lawn mower engine, add a chassis, three wheels, some seats and a modified steering device, we have a car of sorts. It will be underpowered, unreliable and, in all probability, none too safe. It would not, in normal circumstances, meet Department of Transport standards and would be relegated to pottering around the garden. Much the same can be said for modifying a piece of software that was not designed to meet the new purpose. Cars are designed to meet certain performance standards from the moment they are envisaged; there is therefore a continuity in aim as regards the finished product.

We contend that the same can be said of page composition systems. Their roots may lie in the concept of text manipulation, but the orientation towards the final goal must be inherent in the design from day one. It is thus the generic page composition packages that will continue to dominate, until such time as wp software vendors effectively rewrite, rather than modify, their offerings.

Borderline products

Several new products are emerging that are 'borderline' in so far as they represent substantial rewrites of their predecessors or are developed with the wp/DTP market in mind. The latter can be said to result from two strategies. Firstly, there is the need to satisfy the corporate user with an office automation policy already in place. The assumption, which conflicts with that adhered to by DEC and Apple, is that this category of user will not want to 'go the whole hog' in the electronic publishing sphere, but will be content with high-quality output of integrated text and graphics. Secondly, there are those packages that attempt to provide the 'total solution' and, in so doing, run the risk of becoming Jacks of all trades and masters of none.

To elucidate, it may assist to provide examples of software packages that conform to the classification of enhanced wordprocessing; in addition, we will examine others that fall between the two stools, in an attempt to understand how appropriately they fit into the total desktop publishing scene.

Wordcraft Elite

Wordcraft Elite is offered as an enhancment to Wordcraft version 3, a flexible wordprocessing package aimed at the office user. Wordcraft software is supplied with the Canon desktop publishing system, running on the Canon A200 EX IBM-compatible PC AT. Not surprisingly, a Canon laser printer, the LBP-8 A2, completes the bundle.

Wordcraft Elite offers improvements over the original system. It offers all the functions of Wordcraft 3 wordprocessing, which include: 100,000 word spelling checker (user-editable), sophisticated calculation facility, mailmerge, reuseable phrase storage option, better-than-average search and replace, left and right headers and footers, automatic pagination, widow and orphan control and hyphenation prompts ... all in all a versatile wordprocessing package.

Wordcraft Elite provides its own ImageMaster program to make up pages of text and graphics. Text is recalled in the form of wordprocessed files and is displayed on the screen as a text map (or greek, as it is commonly known), i.e. one is presented with little blocks representing the outlines of the text. One can select 'edit mode', which shows a portion of the page and allows the normal wp features to take over. At this level, thankfully, text is text, and not a text 'map' as in the total page preview feature.

Graphics can be placed at the text map stage, hence at no time can the user preview an entire page combining text and graphics.

Wordcraft is a WYSIWYG package at wp level, but not at page make-up level. (It would be more helpful if it were the other way round!) The implication is, therefore, that all typeface conditions, including style and size, must be established and saved at wp level. Subsequent amendments, the necessity for which may only become apparent at output stage, mean a return to the wp environment.

Lastly, full hyphenation and justification, leading, and kerning are not supported, nor is any page description language. Wordcraft has still some way to go before it can boast a viable DTP product.

Samna IV

Samna offers a range of wordprocessing packages that cover needs at various levels of sophistication. The higher-level versions were offering columnar support, basic line diagrams and a text map page preview facility long before the much-vaunted desktop publishing revolution.

It comes as no suprise, therefore, to witness Samna attempting to break into the desktop publishing market. With a well established corporate user base, Samna intends to capitalise on existing devotees who require a publishing facility.

Samna is not a WYSIWYG package. It operates in the MS-DOS environment, without recourse to a GEM or Windows-like user interface.

Text styles such as bold, underline, double underline, and sub and superscript cannot be shown on screen as they will appear on the printed page. Colour monitors display font styles in different colours, which is a helpful indicator but far from perfect.

Pitch vs. point

The main criticism of Samna IV, as far as desktop publishing is concerned, is that points are not used as measurements. The focus appears to be on users of dot matrix or daisywheel printers. Pitch may be set between 5 and 20; point size cannot be defined, unless one is prepared to go to the trouble of performing the appropriate conversions. Hence the daisywheel standard of varying line spacing is 1/48 inch, compared to the traditional printing standard of points measured in 1/72 inch. Currently, neither the Apple LaserWriter nor any PDL is supported.

Desktop publishing features

A Samna page can support up to 10 columns and a limited dictionary. Hyphenation is provided, or discretionary hyphenation may be used. Justification must be specified, since Samna will default to left alignment. There is a rather nebulous 'proportional space check' which does the best it can, but with no facility for interword or intercharacter spacing control, documents will tend to show a 'rivering' of white space. This is obviously not aesthetically pleasing.

Graphics integration

Samna can accept business graphics: charts and graphs created under Samna's Decision Graphics can be placed directly into the document. As in earlier releases, the facility exists for producing simple graphics – rules and boxes – on screen.

Samna Word IV is a very powerful wordprocessing package that includes many options over and above those normally found on a standard wp package. Most impressive is the Word Base Manager (available with Samna IV Plus), which allows words and phrases to be located and retrieved on a multifile basis. It then prints a report listing line and page number, file name, and directory name. Index generation and a 'math' mode are useful additions.

NEW SAMNA WORD IV . . .

THE FIRST STEP TO DESKTOP PUBLISHING !

Publishing Power
and
Ease of Use

New *SAMNA WORD IV* - can offer the user of a laser printer unbridled **Publishing** capabilities. These extremely powerful features are extremely easy to use.

Fast...Powerful
and
Versatile

Speed and power.

New *SAMNA WORD IV* offers the user increased speed by allowing selective writing to disk.
New *SAMNA WORD IV* delivers high power word processing features like **on-screen columns, graphics and text integration.**
You can use *SAMNA WORD IV* to create news letters, fliers, reports, etc. Chose from a variety of fonts.
Select from *30 different* type styles, sizes and weights at any *one* time!

DOWNLOADABLE FONTS
TO LASER PRINTERS
TO EGA CARDS
Because of our special **development agreement** with *Hewlett Packard* we support all of *259* fonts available with the LaserJet Plus or the 500 Plus

New Graphics
and
Text Integration

Figures, charts and Graphs can be placed directly into your document. No more Cutting and Pasting to produce documents like this one.

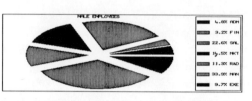

No other graphics software gives you over 30 built-in calculations, plus the power to add your own.

SAMNA's new DECISION GRAPHICS is ultra smart. Ultra simple. Ultra fast. A few easy keystrokes and suddenly boring numbers make beautiful sense. Rather than spending time working on your computer, Your computer can be working for you.

For those users requiring a full Greek alphabet and special technical maths extended symbols on a PC which has an EGA card installed. No more limitations imposed by the IBM character set.

Samna
Decision graphics
And Samna Word IV

A Beautiful Match

SAMNA's new DECISION GRAPHICS is ultra smart. Ultra simple. Ultra fast.

Over 50 New
Features Described
Please review the attached document for a detailed explanation of the **more than 50 new powerful and productive features** that have been added to SAMNA WORD IV.

If you think that your users can benefit from **Samna** and **Samna Decision Graphics** then don't wait ...

Buy today, ask the professionals, IBM, DEC, Hewlett-Packard, AT&T, TI, Philips, Ferranti, and Sharp, for details.

Fig. 8.1 Sample using Samna Word IV Plus.

Undoubtedly, the MS-DOS-based desktop publisher can benefit from using Samna. However, its place in the production of a finished document must remain fairly and squarely in the field of text entry. Samna offers very little in the way of high-quality output support, and only limited typographical features and graphics integration. It may suffice for the production of in-house reports, but cannot realistically be slotted into the classification of page layout software. Samna files can be output in both ASCII and DCA format. It therefore makes an ideal bedfellow for packages such as Xerox's Ventura.

Microsoft Word version 3.0 – Macintosh-based

Even early versions of Microsoft Word permitted the Macintosh user to make use of PostScript and the RIP for high-quality output in true industry standard fonts. Indeed, we know of several innovative users who have produced long publications, including manuals and reference books, using Microsoft Word alone.

It is not just the addition of a columnar facility that changes a wp package into a page composition package overnight. A very large proportion of publications never need layout in columns It is the typographical precision and quality of output that is the key. Microsoft Word version 1.05 proved adequate for document production; version 3.0, with a wealth of enhancements, may well prove to be one of the few wp packages to successfully 'cross the line'.

Wordprocessing functions
Word allows 16 'windows' or files to be opened simultaneously – useful if one is doing considerable cutting and pasting from one document to another. The menu system has been improved, allowing novice users a set of primary menus, as in the standard Macintosh environment. A 'toggle' facility reveals the more comprehensive menu options, hence providing different learning levels. Menus are, to a certain extent, user-definable, and can be customised to reveal only those options that are likely to be used.

Text attributes
New text attributes not included in the old version include: double underscore, dotted underscore, strikeout, all caps, small caps and hidden. The latter permits the insertion of PostScript commands for direction to the printer. All standard Adobe-supplied fonts are supported, be they resident in the PostScript device or downloadable.

Page formatting/graphics support
Word version 3.0 allows up to six columns per page. MacPaint graphics can be placed on the page, and borders, boxes and rules can be produced. Those ready and able to get to grips with PostScript can produce almost unlimited graphic effects, while those unprepared to go to such lengths can make use of a rudimentary macro language that permits production of simple graphics for incorporation in the page.

An extremely useful new tool is the enhanced preview facility that displays two pages side by side. Dotted lines indicating margins can be moved and stretched, causing the text to reformat automatically to accommodate the area change. Page preview allows repositioning of headers, footers and page numbers, thus even though a style sheet type approach has been implemented, individual pages can still be modified.

On the subject of style sheets, Word offers a very simple facility referred to as 'outlines'. This is a capable tool for reorganising long documents, and the package is supplied complete with nine modifiable document outlines – a useful aid for the novice user.

Typographical functions

Word makes no claim to anything other than wordprocessing status, though it does claim to be one of the most comprehensive packages available. The level of sophistication offered for the professional setting of type is therefore restricted.

Specific desktop publishing application software

The majority of true composition packages examined in earlier chapters are aimed at two types of publication: long documents of a general nature, where most pages will conform, in the main, to the same layout and typeface attributes; and publications such as newsletters, where each page will be unique in some respect. We have made it clear that the division is not rigid, and one type of package can be successfully utilised to produce almost any kind of publication.

An industry standard has emerged that allows simple classification of page make-up systems. Deviations from those standards may be greeted with scepticism, despite a niche for more esoteric software.

In the personal computer industry, where average application package costs are low, the user can afford to purchase specialist software for specialist applications. MacAuthor and Lotus Manuscript were written with specific areas of publishing in mind, and are not the results of 'bricolage'. The features offered are therefore relevant to the target user group.

MacAuthor – Macintosh based

MacAuthor, as the name implies, was designed with the writer in mind; indeed, it is currently being used as a wordprocessing package that also generates camera-ready copy. We have established, on numerous

THE TEMPEST

SCENE I . *On a ship at sea ; a tempestuous noise of thunder and lightning heard.*

Enter a SHIPMASTER *and a* BOATSWAIN.

MASTER. Boatswain !

BOATS. Here, master ; what cheer?

MASTER. Good! Speak to th' mariners ; fall to't yarely, or we run ourselves aground ; bestir, bestir.   [*Exit.*

Enter MARINERS.

BOATS. Heigh, my hearts ! cheerly, cheerly, my hearts ! yare, yare ! Take in the topsail. Tend to the maasters whistle. Blow till thou burst thy wind, if room enough.

Enter ALFONSO, SEBASTION, ANTONIO, FERDINAND, GONZALO, *and* OTHERS

ALON. Good boatswain, have care. Where's the master ? Play the men.

BOATS. I pray now, keep below.

ANT. Where is the master boson ?

BOATS. Do you not here him? You mar our labour; keep your cabins; you do assist the storm.

GON. Nay, good, be patient.

BOATS. When the sea is. Hence! What cares these roarers for the name of king? To cabin ! Silence! Trouble us not.

GON. Good, yet remember whom thou hast aboard.

BOATS. None that I love more than myself. You are counsellor; if you can command these elements to silence, and work the peace of the present, we will not hand a rope more. Use your authority; if you cannot , give thanks you have liv'd so long and make yourself ready in your cabin for the mischance of the hour, if it so hap. - Cheerily, good hearts! - Out of our way, I say.   [*Exit*

GON. I have great comfort from this fellow. Methinks he hath no drowning mark upon him; his complection is perfect gallows. Stand fast, good Fate, to his hanging; make the rope of his destiny our cable, for our own doth little advantage. If he be not born to be hang'd our case is miserable.   [*Exeunt*

Re-enter BOATSWAIN.

BOATS. Down with the topmast. Yare, lower, lower! Bring her to try wi' th' maincourse. [*A cry within*] A plague upon theis howling! They are louder than the weather or our office.

Re-enter SEBASTION, ANTONIO, *and* GONZALO

Fig. 8.2   Sample of a MacAuthor document output on an Apple LaserWriter.

occasions, that the great majority of Macintosh software supports PostScript, and MacAuthor is no exception.

A British product, MacAuthor was developed as a direct result of frustration at not being able to find software suitable for writing needs. It holds special appeal for the script writer, in so far as the set-up options are ideal for typical script layouts. (See Fig. 8.2 for sample of MacAuthor output.)

MacAuthor works on the basis of frames and 'paragraph styles'. Frames can be created within frames, ad infinitum, and are designated for either text or graphics. The paragraph style option allows the creation of a basic boilerplate specifying font, point size, style, indent, etc. This is then named and automatically added to the appropriate pull down-menu.

Columns vs. boxes
Let us assume that the example in Fig. 8.2 is actually being created. Text would be entered freely and at speed, probably in the default Macintosh font, Geneva. When a scene was completed, the author would then define which areas, or blocks, required a specific style. In this case, three styles have been predefined as suitable definitions for the character's name, the actual dialogue, and instructions pertaining to actions, stage positions etc.

The reason that MacAuthor is successful where all others fail is that it is not column based. If we were to attempt to achieve the same end with, say, PageMaker, we would have to use tabs; this would slow down input considerably and would not allow wordwrap of the discrete areas. Conversely, the use of columns would necessitate the creation of text in three distinct chunks, since text flows down columns not across them. There is, moreover, no guarantee that once the separate files (i.e. for character, dialogue and instructions) had been placed, the columns would read across correctly. The probability is that character A would be reading character B's lines, while performing character C's actions.

MacAuthor is one of the few packages that successfully combine wordprocessing with page layout facilities. It is specialised, and does not purport to be a general purpose tool; but because it was envisaged and developed from scratch, it performs the desired function well.

Lotus Corporation's Manuscript – MS-DOS-based

Yet another package conceived and developed for the more specialised user, Manuscript, like MacAuthor, combines text entry with page layout. The product's focus is very much on the technical user who may wish to produce reports or manuals. Given that a maximum document size of approximately 800 pages is supported (depending, primarily, on the mix of text and graphics), it is well suited to the latter.

Manuscript overcomes the page vs. document question by providing two modes of use; 'structured', which allows a style sheet facility to be evoked, and 'unstructured', which allows pages to be built up bit by bit. The package allows import of ASCII and DCA files, as well as files from Lotus 1-2-3 and Symphony. Tables can be integrated into the page, as can business graphics.

Manuscript offers some interesting facilities such as spelling checker, word count, and automatic generation of table of contents, table of tables and table of figures. A document revision comparison checks word by word throughout the file and highlights any amendments.

Typical desktop publishing features

Manuscript offers as much typographical sophistication as some of the dedicated page layout systems mentioned: micro-justification, hyphenation and widow and orphan control, global document formats allowing for title, left and right pages, scanned image support (TIFF files) and, perhaps of most significance, PostScript support. A WYSIWYG preview feature allows the made-up page to be displayed, thankfully in readable rather than 'text map' form.

Manuscript may, unwittingly perhaps, have paved the way for a generation of 'task specific' composition systems. As long as standards are maintained, and the importance of PDLs – and, by extension, the output of true fonts – is realised, this development can only serve to further the cause.

The market diversifies

Having defined, early on, our criteria for an acceptable desktop publishing system, it should be clear that enhanced wordprocessing has still some way to go. Yet the traditional PC user, while developing more typographical know-how and more sophisticated demands, has always been cost conscious. Witness the annual rate at which PC dealers have, because of cut-throat discounting, gone out of business.

Given such diverse approaches – i.e. the policy of short-term saving (epitomised by those who decide against the purchase of a PostScript device and then run into trouble when they wish to output to a typesetter) vs. the long-term planner who realises the benefit of coexistence with the world of high-resolution output – certain distinct levels of 'publishing' system are emerging.

Some business sectors freely admit that they do not require industry standard fonts, have no intention of outputting to a typesetter, and wouldn't understand hyphenation and justification if they had it. These constitute, in the main, businesses that have until recently been dependent on typewriters or rudimentary wp.

The main criteria in opting for high-quality output are to raise company profile, ensure greater readability of publications, and keep abreast of the competition. Prime candidates would be building contractors, solicitors and surveyors. These companies 'publish' a considerable volume of printed material, often of poor quality, with the inevitable manual corrections, poorly aligned text, and no supporting diagrams or plans other than costly hand-produced drafts.

The typical user in this bracket certainly wouldn't be concerned with the technicalities of Bitstream vs. ITC fonts. What he should be concerned with is ease of use. In general, it is enhanced wp software that presents limitations on text and graphics integration, true WIMPs environments and WYSIWYG representations. Moreover, a system that requires embedded control codes to inform the printer of changes in font attributes (such as would be the case if using a standard wordprocessing package with the Hewlett Packard LaserJet) could not lay claim to ease of use.

Chapter Nine
Who Does What in Desktop Publishing

There are many questions to be asked and answered, such as: 'Why do I want to become a desktop publisher?' 'How can I profit from desktop publishing?' 'What is involved in desktop publishing?' 'What is the publishing process, and how is a publication designed?' 'How do I go about getting a manual, newsletter, or annual report printed, bound and distributed? To answer these, it is useful to look at the tasks involved in both desktop and traditional publishing. The same tasks or activities have to be carried out irrespective of the method used.

A desktop publisher, like any publisher, is responsible for all the activities involved in creating a document and distributing it to its eventual readers. This includes the coordination of all the publishing functions to ensure that each activity is completed on time, according to established standards, and at a predetermined level of cost. Some of these functions may be performed by others (editors or printers, for example) but, whoever does them, someone has to be responsible for the entire project.

Regardless of who performs the various functions, the traditional publishing process usually requires a number of clearly defined activities to be performed. Desktop publishing is no different and will mean that, in some cases, these activities could be as diverse as authorship, page layout, graphics and even selling. Therefore many skills have to be developed if all the activities are to be carried out by a single individual.

Even if there are a number of people in the team, the coordinator will have to understand all the activities. This requires a basic understanding of the traditional publishing process – a process that is not difficult to grasp, though perhaps a bit mysterious for those who have never seen how publications are produced. Once the stages through which a manuscript progresses and the importance of each stage to the success of the publication are understood it will become obvious that desktop publishing projects present a challenging but manageable activity.

Identifying the audience

A desktop publisher must first identify the target audience, and then choose the authors and topics that will capture that audience. The text, whether it be a business report, an article or a book-length manuscript, must be written, edited and shaped to suit the audience or market. If the document is not designed to suit the tastes of the target audience, there is a real danger that it will not be read.

Decisions also have to be made about the physical shape of the document. This means the final trim size, page lengths and widths, number of pages, printing processes, type of paper and style of binding. These are all aspects that affect the image of the publication. The publication, if it is badly bound, with ill-fitting type, will not make a good impact, however important and well written the text.

Publications must be produced in quantities determined by the size of the audience. There is nothing more soul-destroying than to be left with a stack of unwanted publications. Not only is it bad for the ego; it is bad for the image of the magazine or publication. If the printing venture is to be successful, you must determine the balance of each project's potential. Even non-profit-making publications must be supervised so that expenses remain within limits.

In order to get a feel for the size of the market, it is helpful if some time is spent promoting and distributing the publication.

The publisher as planner

A desktop publisher wears many hats during the project, and takes responsibility for the whole process to ensure that it does not falter along the way. A more detailed look at the publishing process will reveal the magnitude of the responsibility that has to be undertaken by the desktop publisher.

The roles are explained in terms of the traditional publishing process. The roles that a desktop publisher assumes will depend upon individual abilities and resourcefulness. However, at each stage help is available, if needed, in the form of freelance, independent professionals.

A publisher is a planner who can see a project in his mind's eye and know how all the parts will fit. A lot of planning has to be done before a single word is set on paper. A publisher has to draw on or develop literary, artistic, technical, promotional and commercial skills.

Depending on the type of publication to be created, artistic and literary skills may take precedence over promotional and commercial ones, or vice versa. Again, it is important to understand the market at which the publication is aimed. The publisher must be concerned with the personal vision and creativity that goes into the publishing project as much as with paying bills, collecting invoices, distribution and advertising.

If a publication is to survive as an on-going affair, it is important to adhere to a strict budget. This means that financial resources must be available to ensure that money gets into the right hands when needed.

Working alone or with colleagues, the desktop publisher is the driving force of the publication and leader of the project. If you are a desktop publisher in a corporate environment, your chief concern might well be getting the right information to the target audience within a justifiable and agreed budget. Promotion and sales would take a back seat in this environment whereas, with a profit-making publication, promotion and sales are crucial to the whole endeavour. The desktop publisher, like any other publisher, has to reflect the needs of the market and lead the project team in the correct direction.

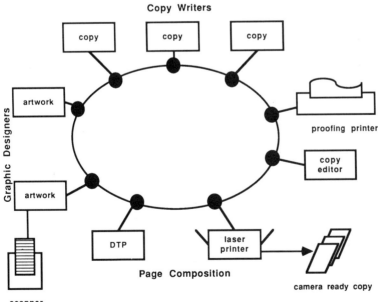

Fig. 9.1 The desktop publishing circle.

Like any other publisher, the desktop publisher must make many important decisions. In the business of publishing, the decision to publish involves a commitment of money, time and effort. The publisher has to plan how a publication will be produced and manufactured, how it will look, how much it will cost, and when it is to be completed. All this requires experience, and even experienced publishers can and do make mistakes. However experienced or inexperienced the desktop publisher may be, there is no substitute for researching and planning before a project gets underway.

The writer – temperamental but necessary

The writer or author creates the textual contents of the publication. Writers often have an inflated image of their own importance and can, on occasion, be very tiresome. This is because they often want to be involved in all the other aspects of publishing. Although the writer may be an authority on a given subject, it is a combination of people or skills that are responsible for creating the message.

In many cases, of course, the writer will also be the desktop publisher. However, for most commercial publications it is important to contact other writers to produce the basic copy for publication.

In the production of company manuals, documentation or newsletters, other employees may be the main source of information, although the staff writers must secure information from them through interviews or written reports. On the other hand, if the publication is of a literary nature, the main source of copy may be poets, short-story writers, novelists or non-fiction writers.

Whatever the subject, research of the topic and writing are the responsibility of the writer, who must also meet scheduled deadlines. Today, a writer who uses a wordprocessor also takes on the task of typing, correcting and formulating documents into final form before submitting them to an editor. Who writes for a publication, what topics to cover, and what can and cannot be published are all decisions that the desktop publisher must take.

Desktop publications come in many forms and can carry news, features, letters to the editor, technical questions and answers, photographs, graphs, essays, business columns, memoires, and other items. Although the writers come from many sources, the publisher decides the editorial content of the desktop publication; the writer then executes the decisions of the publisher. In a desktop publishing environment, the writer may be someone of experience or authority and the publisher may be someone less senior. However, in these cases, the publisher must remember who is in charge!

The editor - an unsung hero

In a traditional printing environment, the writer hands over the finished manuscript to an editor. Even if you are the only person in the desktop publishing team, you should not be the editor of your own writing since a degree of objectivity is required. However, there is a need to develop some editorial skills. The editor functions as a quality controller who works closely with the publisher and writer to determine the shape and direction of the manuscript. Editors also have to ensure that the manuscript meets an agreed set of standards. The editor reads the manuscript, checking the clarity, readability, coherence, and organisation.

If there are problems in writing style or content, the editor asks the author for revisions or makes revisions directly to the manuscript. The editor checks the manuscript's completeness and passes it to other readers to check its accuracy or to check that it meets the needs of the readership. The editor determines the number and position of illustrations; sees that front and back matter, such as the table of contents or the index, are prepared; checks article titles, subheadings and bibliographical information; and determines the scheduling of production before sending the manuscripts to the copy editor for final polishing.

For many publications that are produced weekly or monthly, the editor determines fees for articles and discusses with writers the content of the present and future issues. If workloads get too heavy, a desktop publisher can always contact outside editors to help meet deadlines.

The copy editor

The editor gives the manuscript to the copy editor, who picks over the writing with a fine-tooth comb. The copy editor is generally responsible for making sure that the writing style is consistent with the general style of the publication and that the manuscript contains no errors in grammar, spelling, word use, and so on. The copy editor checks for consistency in format of text and captions and use of terminology and, in some cases, verifies facts, names and dates. The copy editor may also initially prepare the manuscript for production by marking all content that is not straight text, such as tables, phrases in italics, figure captions, chapter headings, subheadings and footnotes, with codes that match the designer's type specification.

Copy editing a manuscript is a detailed job that requires concentration and accurate adherence to established standards. It is the indispensable stage of quality assurance. It is often a task that is overlooked when only one or two people are involved in desktop publishing. This is a mistake; it may be a dry and not very glamorous job, but it has to be done. If it is not, mistakes and inconsistencies creep in and the publication looks amateurish. This can mean that a lot of hard work and effort are wasted.

A publication is only as strong as its weakest link: always make sure that copy editing tasks are done, and done well.

The art director and designer

Page after page of unbroken text makes for bleak reading. It is important to create a publication that is interesting to look at as well as to read. It does not matter if it is a one-page report or a large publication: it must hold the reader's interest. This means that the principals of good design are needed, and if the task falls to the sole desktop publisher he or she will have to conjure up some of the artist within.

The publication's art director sets the overall tone and direction of the artwork and design of the publication. The designer creates the actual specification for size, space, typefaces, headings, illustrations, and each special element in the publication. Sometimes the art director and the designer are the same person.

A good designer will strike a pleasing balance between illustrations and text. Placing well-designed charts, illustrations and photographs throughout a document gives a sense of pace and vitality to a publication. In short, the design must help the text communicate with the audience.

The art director ensures that high-quality illustrations and artwork are used in the publication. Illustrations require consistent style, good technical quality, focal points of interest, and clarity. The art director creates the look, tone and feeling of a document in order to make the desired impression on the reader. The designer of the document is concerned with page layout, the placement of the headings, the use of different typefaces, the publication's size, the space between the lines, margins, captions, page numbers, and so forth. By laying out pages with a specific style, the designer can make them distinctive and sophisticated, or open and friendly, as appropriate.

Designing a document requires knowledge of, and experience with, the principals of form, space, texture and colour. The designer and art director are required to have an understanding of typesetting and printing, to anticipate the final printed output, and to ensure that it is achieved.

Traditionally, designing pages and layout artwork required the designer to create mechanical camera-ready copy of the final pages as they would be printed. Mechanicals are created by ruling an artboard to the prescribed page size and pasting the illustrations and text in place in accordance with the designer's specification.

Since the mechanicals are eventually photographed to produce printing plates, creating them is a highly skilled and exacting task. Fortunately for the desktop publisher, the difficulty of producing mechanicals is reduced by the use of page layout software. The labour-intensive layout of the publication on the board is, for the most part, unnecessary. Using desktop publishing or page layout software, it is possible to arrange final text and illustrations on the computer screen according to a specification, and output to a printer. It is this element of desktop publishing that makes it possible for a comparative novice to produce quality documents at a fraction of the cost traditionally associated with the task.

The artist's skills

The artist creates the final artwork from the writer's or author's rough sketches. Some publications do not require artwork, and the publisher has considerable flexibility in how much or how little artwork is used. In many cases, it is the budget and the time available that are the restricting factors. Although the paint and draw software packages available to the desktop publisher reduce the cost of creating artwork, it is often the imagination of the desktop publisher that is the limiting factor.

Artists, designers and art directors, are specialists. If you are a sole desktop publisher, it is likely that you will have to develop artistic skills; however, graphic programs for personal computers help in the creation of camera-ready artwork. As with other publishing activities, it is possible to hire artists on a job-by-job basis. It must be borne in mind, however, that artists with different styles will create different effects within the publication.

The production supervisor

Most desktop publishers have to assume the role of production supervisor. The production supervisor is responsible for transforming the final copy-edited manuscript into a printed and bound document within a specified budget. The production supervisor coordinates the stages of the production process and prevents undue delays. All the steps of the process – composing text, proofreading text, making up pages, checking page proofs, preparing indexes, inserting corrections, printing and binding – are directed by the production supervisor.

The production supervisor finds suppliers – outside experts and craftsmen, such as designers, printers and binders – who contract to produce the publication. Decisions must be made about the type of binding necessary, the quality of the paper to be used, and delivery dates. The production supervisor secures estimates from suppliers and balances the needs of the organisation, keeping production costs low and maintaining a healthy profit margin if the publication is profit orientated.

Generally, the production supervisor is concerned with two types of costs: plant costs and manufacturing costs.

Plant costs are an expense that occurs once. For the traditional publishing environment, this item would include the costs of typesetting, proofs, illustrations, page make-up and printing plates. In the desktop publishing environment, these activities still have to be paid for; yet since the methods are different, they cost less in most situations.

Manufacturing costs involve paper, printing and binding, and vary with the number of copies you print.

Typesetting

From the time of Gutenberg, who invented the movable-type printing press in 1450, to the latter half of the nineteenth century, type was set by hand. Setting type by hand required that each character be packed into a composing stick and assembled in lines in a tray called a galley. The galley tray was placed in a press and inked. The paper was positioned over the press, and pressed against the type to produce the printed page.

Around 1890, the linotype machine was invented to automate the setting of type. The operator sat and typed at the keyboard of a large machine, holding matrices or moulds representing letters to drop into place, thus forming lines of type. Molten metal was forced over the type to create a slug, which was in turn placed in a galley tray. This time-consuming method of typesetting has been largely replaced by speedier methods of phototypesetting and computerising cold type systems.

With phototypesetting, the machine generates images of text and characters and projects them on to film, which is used to expose photosensitive plates. These sophisticated machines use four basic elements: a source of light for generating images, the character image that represents the type font, the optical system for projecting the text image, and the phototypesetting material that captures the image. Essentially, the machine produces photographs of typeset text that are transferred to plates without any metal being cast. The product is usually a long, page-width column of text that has not yet been paginated, called a galley proof.

Cold type composing systems, like the desktop publisher's personal computer system, enable the compositer to sit at a terminal and work at a keyboard to compose a printed page. With a cold type system like the Linotronic 300, the electronic signals from the keyboard reproduce and imprint words in black type on white proof sheets in the line length and typeface selected by the art director. The proof sheets are proofed, corrected, cut up, pasted on to mechanical camera-ready copy, and photographed to produce printing plates. Your page layout software allows you to avoid the physical cutting and pasting procedure called make-up. Page make-up is done electronically on a computer screen.

The great advantage of personal computer page-composition systems and laser printing is that you need not have a compositor re-enter, or compose, the publication by hand. You save the expense of skilled labour.

The proof reader

In the traditional production process, the compositer sets out the galley or page proofs and returns them to the publisher for checking. The proof reader reads the material carefully, comparing the original copy-edited manuscript with the typeset version produced by the composi-tor. On the lookout for such things as letter transposition, mis-spelling, page numbering which is out of sequence, misplaced or omitted lines of text, broken characters, and failure to follow type specification, the proof reader tries to catch errors before they are published for all to see.

Although time-consuming, proofreading a document and making corrections before handing it over to the printer is an unavoidable and necessary step. Few things undermine the credibility and authority of a publication more than typographical errors.

In the desktop publishing environment, the need for a proof reader is reduced since all text, once typed into the system, is transferred from one system to another by the disk-to-disk method. However, there are often gremlins in the system, and a final proof-read is therefore well worth the effort.

The paste-up artist

Corrected galleys and completed artwork come together to be paged on boards, or camera-ready mechanicals. The person who does this in the traditional printing process may be the designer or a person who is skilled at layout and paste-up techniques performed on a drafting board. The paste-up artist cuts the galleys and pastes them into pages, allowing space for illustrations, running heads and footers, marginal text and display text, and all the special elements. The design specifications are adhered to with precision. Nevertheless, many individual decisions about photo or art placement, special type or spacing must be made because the design specification cannot account for every contingency encountered in laying out a multi-page document.

In desktop publishing, layout can be done with the special page composition software already discussed.

The printer

The camera-ready mechanicals of the publication are sent to the printer. You will usually not venture to take on the role of printing multiple copies of your publication unless photocopy quality and page quantity are all you need. Printing equipment is costly, the printing process is complex, and printing set-up requires highly specialised skills.

The printer transfers the image from the mechanicals to the film, and then to printing plates, and finally to multiple printed copies, most probably using a method called lithographic offset printing. For offset printing, mechanicals are mounted on a camera board and photographed to produce negatives. The film is used to transfer the images of the document on to a thin, photosensitive metal sheet used as a printing plate. Offset printing uses the plate carrying the image of your

The Fake Horse

A professor invented a mechanical horse which had a jet packs on its flanks and roller skates on its feet which made it win races every time.

Meanwhile, on the other side of town a gang of crooks were plotting. The names of the crooks were Jack, Sack, Jim, Pinch, Lolly, Loot and Tessie Take. They saw a picture of the horse in a newspaper and decided to steal it.

They jump on there motor bikes and rode away to the laboratory. When they got there they had some sandwiches and a cup of tea. The professor forget to lock the door so they did not have to break in.

They tied everybody up including the Jocky whose name was Rachel May Apple Horse Mad. Then the gang jumped on the horse and gallop away.

After an hour the professor got untied and phoned the police and they went after the gang and the horse.

The police gave a long chase. It start like this, in and out of side streets and round Bean Road. They knock over and sent them fling everywhere.

But Then The Horse Broke Down!!!! The Police flew straight past them, so the robbers got away with the fake horse and were very happy.

THE END by Leah Bate

age 10.

Fig. 9.2 Example of a story keyed in directly by a child, showing the use of DTP in education.

publication to transfer ink to the page.

Roles for the desktop publisher

As can be seen, the cycle of actions to produce a finished publication using the traditional method is no different in the desktop publishing method. The way in which events in the cycle are carried out differs and therefore the importance of the individual parts vary from one method to the other.

In both situations, the publisher has to understand the market and how to attract its attention, and to take overall control of the process. The text has to be well researched and written, edited carefully, proof read, laid out with flair and style, printed on the correct paper, bound or put together in order, and distributed to the target audience. The personal computer, with the relevant software, helps a great deal in many of these activities, but does not do them automatically.

The desktop publisher still has to learn a range of skills and, unlike the specialists in the traditional publishing environment, is unlikely to be able to focus on one or two of them. Desktop publishing can be a rewarding and exciting activity, but it will never be as simple as just loading a software program into the computer.

Chapter Ten
Designing Pages for Publication

The purpose of any publication, whether it be a book, newsletter, report, journal, proposal, or advertisement, is to communicate information. In order to communicate, the publication has to draw the reader towards it. This attraction often has to do with style and page layout. Planning the pages to achieve a special purpose draws attention to your printed idea, directs the reader's eye to key points and facts, and distinguishes your publication from others with a similar purpose. Whether you use the page layout software discussed in this book, or revert to the traditional publishing process, or use a combination of the two systems, you should become familiar with the elements of page design. In many cases, it is better not to publish than to publish badly.

Putting ideas across effectively has as much to do with page design and layout as with writing itself. If words are the written language of a publication, then design is its body language. There is a science and an art to good design, and learning the principals of good page design takes time. Design is a crucial step in the publishing process that affects all subsequent steps, as well as the cost and ultimate effectiveness of the communication.

Since the page layout software available on the personal computer is still in its infancy, many elements of the design tool box are missing. There are limitations in the types of font that are offered and in the hyphenation and justification of the text. Nevertheless, the programs discussed in this book are very innovative and exciting. They demonstrate the directions that have been taken in page layout software for personal computers. As this field develops, we can expect to see more sophisticated professional products that are easier for the novice to use. For the foreseeable future, however, the skills associated with traditional page design will have to be learnt and understood.

Elements of page design

Page design is a science and an art, combining many elements to one effect. A well designed page uses principles and techniques of balance, contrast, focal points, consistency and organisation to present information in an interesting and clear manner. Designing a page requires attention to detail in order to interrelate space, size, colour, shape, shading, graphics and typefaces. A single design often calls for hundreds of tiny decisions and specifications.

White space

White space is the basic element used to compose a page; the other elements, such as body text, graphics, headings, rules, lines and page numbers, occupy this space. Black type in white space, for example, draws the eye.

How large the page is, and how much of it is devoted to type, affects the reader. Long lines of text are harder to read than short lines. This is why newspapers prefer to set out their information in short lines.

Large or bold type stands out and draws the attention of the reader. Again, newspapers have been using this technique with their headlines for generations. However, if too many elements stand out, they clash with each other and clutter the look. On the other hand, uninterrupted text is often visually boring – it might be cheap to produce, but it is dull to read.

The designer must specify how each element is to use the white space: that is, every item that you see on the page of a publication must be sized and placed exactly. In many desktop publishing situations, the designer will also be the publisher, editor, paste-up artist, proof reader, artist and salesman. Even if this is the case, he must still have a good grasp of page layout and design.

Common measures

The common measures used are points and picas. Typically, a designer scours a manuscript to detect all common and special elements that must be sized and placed. These elements are numerous and may include indents, page size, title and half-title pages, copyright page, chapter or article opening pages, table of contents, levels of headings and subheadings, text placement, text font and size, column size, special terms, technical terms, running heads, pagination, lines, boxes, line length, margins, numbered lists, tables, footnotes, graphics, photos, captions and artwork, figure legends, mathematical symbols, computer listings, use of colour screen, glossary, appendix, index and justification.

Mockups
To ensure consistency of design throughout a manuscript and for

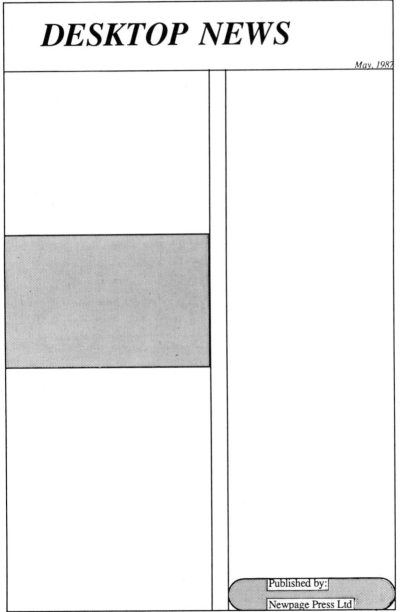

Fig. 10.1 Page mock-up produced using PageMaker.

reference, it is advisable to mockup several pages of the publication to get a feel of how page elements will look when turned into the final product. These sample pages include all the elements of the publication and serve as reference as you lay out pages with your page layout software (see Fig. 10.1). These mockups can be revised many times before they are finalised, according to the required design of the publication.

Along with these specified elements, there must be a keen sense of how to balance them in the white space available in order to achieve the look and tone desired. This might be informal but innovative, or informative and stylish but simple, or whatever. It is this style that will distinguish one publication from another and attract the reader's attention, and one should never underestimate the importance of impact in a publication's ability to communicate. Developing this artistic sensitivity takes experience, study and learning from mistakes.

Graphics

Graphics, in the widest sense, are a particularly important design element because illustrations – photos and artwork – communicate effectively and often occupy a large part of the space in a publication. Furthermore, graphics such as photographs may need to be treated separately in the production process, though in some page make-up programs they can be handled along with the text. Indeed, it is the ability to combine text with graphics that has been instrumental in projecting desktop publishing to its present position. Graphic art may have a wide variety of forms and purpose. Graphics include charts, graphs, photographs, diagrams, freehand or structured drawings, display type, symbols, computer generated art, and cartoons.

Artwork should convey information in a way that is easily understood and retained. Besides being interesting and stimulating, effective graphics reduce the need for extensive explanation, simplify relationships, show comparisons in size and scale, and break textual monotony. A picture can be worth a thousand words. One cartoon may sum up the political situation of a country or the mood of its people in a manner that words – however many – could not.

Key decisions

The key to successful graphics is deciding which central textual ideas need be emphasized through illustrations. Simplicity – that is, narrowing the focus to one idea – is generally an effective approach in developing a graphic that communicates well. It is more effective to hammer home one or two ideas than shower the reader with many.

Costs for graphic art vary widely. Photographs may be free or cost up to £100 for well known photographers. The price of creative art depends on the artist, the complexity of the artwork and the time it takes, but there is a similar price range. If the desktop publisher has an artistic or graphic background, he can generate artwork on a computer and produce images at a fraction of normal costs (see Figs 10.2 and 10.3). In any event, in considering the graphic content of the publication you should include costs because, unless controlled, these can be substantial.

Fig. 10.2 Example of MacPaint illustrations.

Typefaces

A typeface is a complete set of characters, letters, numbers and special symbols. All characters have similar design motifs – that is, their bodies, shape and thickness identify them as being from the font set. A font is the complete set of characters of one typeface needed for composing a document. A typeface family is the sum total of all available styles, such as roman, light, italic, condensed, small caps, strikeout, expanded and bold. The typeface is usually supplied in 6 point to 72 point size.

Hundreds of typeface designs exist, although you may be limited in your choice to a dozen or so, depending on the faces available for your computer printer. Currently, only a limited number of typefaces are available for desktop publishing, compared with the many hundreds of fonts professional typesetters and printers have at their disposal.

Each typeface emphasises a characteristic mood or style – from buoyant, sedate, formal, casual, technical, literary, elegant, and so on. Some typefaces have serifs at the end of the matrix of each letter, and some are sans serif (without the cross line). Some typefaces are easy to read in long lines and large blocks; sans serif typefaces work well in smaller doses, such as in advertising copy, illustration headings, etc. (See Fig. 10.4).

Fig. 10.3 Example of MacPaint, illustrating different effects.

When choosing typefaces and styles, one should be primarily concerned with the overall appearance and legibility. Some typeface designs are not easy to read and are not intended for use in text. Often, these faces are used for large displays, as in chapter or article titles, fliers or advertisements. Italic styles should not be used for normal text but can be used for highlighting special terms. Boldface type should be used sparingly as it draws attention even more than italics. However, boldface is most effective for headings, table headings, captions, special columns or page numbers. Glossary terms, running heads and references are normally produced in italics. Underlining should be avoided.

Changing typeface frequently is a strong temptation for the excited first-time desktop publisher eager to create interesting pages. However, this temptation should be resisted, since it is confusing and difficult for the reader (see Fig. 10.5). Once the typeface has been picked, do not change it without a specific and well considered reason. If there is a requirement to change typeface, style or size, stay with the typeface family to avoid jarring breaks. Always think about the reader's comfort, understanding, and expectation when choosing type for the various elements. Think how you would feel if every time you

This is times a serif font
This is Garamond a serif font
This is Palatino a serif font

This is Helvetica a sans serif font
This is Helvetica condensed light also
a sans serif font
**This Is helvetica condensed black,
you can see this font has no serifs !**

Fig. 10.4 Examples of serif and sans serif fonts.

picked up your daily newspaper the style of printing or the style of type had changed.

Changing point size diminishes or enhances the appearance of the type. Most people comfortably read text set at 10 point. Footnotes and excerpts are usually set a point or two smaller than the body text, as are captions, legends and indexes. Sometimes setting a large amount of peripheral, appendix or reference text in smaller type saves pages, which in turn saves on your printing bill without sacrificing your dignity. You may easily get to grips with the distinguished hierarchy of heading levels by making the most important headings the largest ones. Point size also distinguishes headings and their relative importance in a table of contents, and is a critical factor in all display type larger than normal text – in banners or headlines, for example.

Colour and shading
Colour and shading add much to a publication's appeal, yet the colour alternative is costly. Each additional colour can add between 10 per cent and 25 per cent to the normal printing bill, not to mention the cost of preparation. However, these costs are declining and a good desktop publisher must always be assessing the cost of using colour against the impact it will make.

A less expensive and highly effective way to increase appeal is to use shading. All the software associated with page layout offers this facility: for example, a light grey screen behind a table figure, side bar, chapter opening, etc.

Principles of good page design

In addition to specifying all page elements, there is a need to balance them in the white space available to achieve the desired look and tone. To know what look and tone is required, the publication's purpose must be considered. Newsletters, professional papers, proposals, contracts, updates, articles, short stories, books, brochures and reports all have a different character according to their audience and their intent.

The following list includes some of the principles of good design.

(1) Each design element must be used in a consistent way. If it is specified that special terms appear in italics, all special terms – and nothing else – should be in italics. The typeface chosen for the main body of the text should remain the same for the entire document. The size and level of headings chosen should follow some consistent pattern or hierarchy of presentation. Consistent elements make for smooth transitions, and guide the reader into an easy understanding of the organisation and thought processes of the publication. Inconsistent elements confuse, interrupt and destroy trains of thought, and are a sure sign of inexperience in page layout. Only experienced designers can break rules of consistency without achieving a negative result.

(2) The more elements used in a design, the more variety can be achieved. The corollary to this is that the more variety is achieved, the more visual competition is created – causing interruption, changes in direction and breaks in thought. An increase or decrease in variety can be achieved by the number, organisation or visual weight of design elements used. The variety found in a popular magazine, for example, spices up the publication, makes it interesting and draws readers of different tastes. But a sense of focal point must be maintained, and contrast on the page must serve to highlight the important elements rather than call attention to unimportant ones.

(3) White space is the basic element in attracting the reader's attention. White space is the backdrop canvas on which each element displays itself. Wide margins and ample space focus attention on the elements in the space. Placement of text, graphics and other elements in this white space must be balanced to show each element to best effect. Placing all graphics consistently in one position is sometimes effective, sometimes not. Placing all graphics

near their mention in the text makes it easy for the reader to find them but may create layout problems if the graphics will not fit where they are supposed to.

(4) Design is effective if it goes unnoticed. The reader should not be paying attention to elements in design but to the communication. The elements must be balanced in their white space on the pages, and must harmonise and complement each other. The reader should not have to spend time deciphering the organisation of a page, trying to find where to begin reading or figuring out the logical order of a sequence of graphics. The reader's attention should always be focused on the communication, not on how or why a page was laid out in a particular manner.

(5) Good design is functional. It arises from the needs of the text, serves that text, and enhances its practical use. For example, in a highly referenced publication, page numbers, running heads, tables of contents and index should be carefully designed for the easiest and fastest possible access by the reader, so that information can be found swiftly. In editorial publications, there is a need to design numbered steps and indentations and to distinguish hands-on instructions from general explanatory text. In publications that have illustrations, there is a need to design captions or labels on the illustrations that are simple and clear and do not conspicuously compete for attention with the important elements that the illustration is designed to show. Captions should be arranged consistently and in an organised manner to help the reader understand what is shown in the illustration.

This is not an exhaustive list of design principles, but applying them to the publication can help achieve successful document design. For example, a formal literary look can be achieved by using justified text, large blocks of text and white space, smaller margins, less space between lines, a serif typeface, fewer illustrations, fewer changes in typeface style and, in general, fewer design elements. This approach appeals to the serious or academic readership that already has an interest in the publication's topic and needs little inducement to read it. The emphasis on the textual content and design is simple and straightforward.

An informal or casual look can be achieved by increasing the margins and white space, decreasing line length, and using unjustified text, freehand illustrations, italic headings and running heads, cartoons and more display type.

THE DIFFERENCE BETWEEN ENHANCED WP and DESKTOP PUBLISHING

It is expedient, or so they think, to beef up a wordprocessing package, add a facility for column support, and provide some links with graphics software. The 'piece de resistance" arrives, of course when they develop a page preview facility, and immediately lay claim to the WYSIWYG environment - the panacea for all DTP software. Despite the Heath Robinson approach, success is quaranteed. Or is it?

The demarcation between true page composition systems and enhanced Wordprocessors is currently quite clear to those who have used DTP in anger. Yet, as it means just about anything to anyone, this confuses the issue somewhat. We have attempted above to define DTP as we understand it, and it is based on this understanding that we examine below enhanced wordprocessing, and its limitations to the desktop publisher. We also examine the potential convergence of the two technologies and the resulting implications.

Wordprocessing
The concept of wordprocessing is simple, it is also, a practise so common that we tend to adopt a blase attitude to the benefits of this remarkable innovation, and wonder how we ever lived without it!In essence WP is the manipulation and arrangement

of words.

Unlike using a typewriter,

the words do not go directly onto paper: they appear on a screen which becomes the medium for alterations and edits. Only when the entire document is correct is it commited to paper. In this way a great deal of effort is saved, and the operator is free to work at the full typing speed, since any errors can be put right later. The total saving in time can be quite dramatic, and the final printed output can be free from the ubiquitous typex and manual edits that once had to be endured.
Through the use of wordprocessing, moreover, standard documents can be stored for subsequent editing

and re-use, cutting down on operator time at every re-draft.

The Development of Wordprocessing

The original generation of wordprocessors used special purpose hardware, dedicated to wordprocessing. However, the various components of the system, screen, keyboard, disks, and so on, are the same in principle as those of the personal computer. Today, there is no reason to use such a specialised machine, in preference to the much more flexible PC.

Since the early days of the microcomputer wordprocessing packages have been available. These were once regarded as poor relations of the dedicated wordprocessor with its specialy configured keys that left little room for operator error, or forgotten key strokes. By comparison, WordStar™, as originally implemented

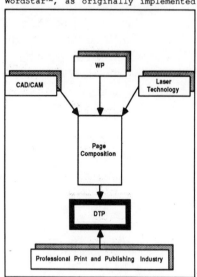

Fig. 10.5 Example of a poorly composed page, using excessive fonts and styles.

Of course, these are not the only ways to achieve a variety of look. With so many elements and ways to use them, the number of design choices is almost limitless. The desktop publisher should not underestimate the impact that design choice will have on a publication and its ability to communicate.

Page layout software

Page layout software is the desktop publisher's most versatile tool for creating and producing a document. These packages integrate word-processing, page design and layout, to replace the traditional paste-up boards. The programs handle graphics and text, change typeface within the document, adjust the size and position of the document's elements, and facilitate the layout of a multitude of publication formats, from newsletters and technical journals to comic books.

Electronic editing functions eliminate the need for the cut-and-paste tools of the trade. Automating this process saves time and production costs, reduces mess, and expands the capability of your computer system. Page layout software packages differ in the sophistication of their features, and the techniques used to implement those features.

It is up to the desktop publisher to analyse page layout requirements and to consider the hardware to be used, the result to be achieved and the resources available. When this is done, a decision can be made on the combination of hardware and software that is needed. No matter what software is used, however, the need for the desktop publisher to understand how to design a page to best effect will always remain.

References

Ashley, R., Fernandez, J. and Samson, B. (1985) *Wordstar Without Tears*. Toronto: Wiley.

Barnard, M. (1986) *Magazine and Journal Production*. London: Blueprint.

Bate, J. St. J. (1987) *The Amstrad PC1512 – A User's Guide*. London: Collins.

Burgess, R. and Bate, J. St. J. (1986) *Office Automation Using the IBM Personal Computer Systems*. London: Collins.

Grout, B., Athanasopoulos, I. and Kutlin, R. (1986) *Desktop Publishing from A to Z*. Berkeley: McGraw-Hill.

Glossary

Access: The ability to retrieve data from a computer storage medium.

Acetate: Transparent sheet of film fixed over camera-ready artwork, which can be developed and used as prepress proofs.

Address: The character or string of characters identifying a unique storage location.

Airbrush: Small compressed-air gun for achieving fine manual ink spraying on artwork.

Algorithm: An arithmetic computer routine in the form of pro-grammed instructions which perform a recurring task.

Alphabet length: Length of a lower-case type font.

Apparent density: Weight of paper per unit of volume.

Application: A program which does a specific task such as account-ing or word processing, rather than a general-purpose program such as an operating system.

Archive: To store data economically off-line for future use in a computer system.

Artwork: Original illustrative copy or typesetting ready for reproduc-tion at prefilm stage.

ASCII: American Standard Code for Information Interchange. A standard way of using the 8 bits of a byte to represent various characters. In ASCII, 7 bits are sufficient to represent the letters of the alphabet, numeric digits, and the main punctuation marks, etc. The remaining bit is used for different purposes in different types of computer.

Author's corrections: Corrections made by the author at proof stage to change the original copy, rather than to rectify literals and other errors made by the typesetter.

Bastard size: Non-standard size of any material or format.

Bit: Binary digit, the smallest possible unit of information. A bit can have only two values (0 or 1 if regarded as a number).

Block: Letterpress printing surface or computer term for a group of bytes.

Bold: Heavier version of a typeface, as distinct from light or medium.

Booting: Loading the operating system, and starting up or resetting the computer.

Bromide: Photographic light-sensitive paper used in photographic reproduction or phototypesetting.

Byte: The smallest unit of information that the computer normally deals with, usually comprising 8 bits, or one character.

Caliper: The thickness of a sheet of paper, measured in microns.

Camera-ready artwork: Typematter or type and line artwork pasted up in position ready for photographing.

Caps: Capital or upper-case letters.

Clean proof: A printer's proof in which there are no errors.

Clicking: Selecting a file or object by using the mouse to locate the pointer over the icon on the screen representing that object, and then pressing the mouse button.

Cluster: An area of disk storage which is the smallest area DOS will allocate to a file – normally 2 sectors (1K).

Combination line and tone: A single print or piece of film combining half-tone and line work.

Compose: To make up type into lines and/or pages.

Condensed type: A typeface with narrow characteristics.

Copy: Material for publication.

Copyright: The proprietary right in a work, as defined by law.

Crop: To cut back part of an illustration, so as to give better effect or to achieve better fit.

Cursor: A mark or pointer shown on the screen that can be moved to the item to be selected.

Daisywheel: A type of printer that uses a print head shaped like a daisy.

Database: A structured collection of data.

DBMS: Database management system.

DIA: Document interchange architecture. A standard defined by IBM for the format of the electronic 'envelope' containing a document.

Dialogue box: A special window opened on the screen by GEM, which asks you a question and allows you to key in the answer.

Disk: Normally a magnetic disk for storing data; either a hard disk or a floppy disk.

Disk drive: The machinery for reading and writing data on disks.

DOS: Disk operating system. The main operating system used on the IBM PC and compatibles.

Double clicking: 'Opening' a file, or other object, by placing the cursor over its icon on the screen and pressing the mouse button twice very quickly.

Dragging: Moving an icon about on the screen by holding down the mouse button while moving the mouse.

Edit: To check, rearrange and correct data or copy before final presentation.

Elite: A small typeface normally associated with typewritten text.

Em: The width of the body of the lower case 'm' in any typeface.

En: Half the width of em.

Face: A style of type.

Fair copy: A correction-free copy of a document.

Family: A group of fonts related to the basic text roman face.

Field: An item of data in a file.

Figure: A line illustration referred to in the text of document.

File: A collection of data on disk, e.g. a wordprocessing document.

Floppy disk: A type of disk that is encased in a protective jacket and can be removed from the computer.

Folder: A WIMPs term, equivalent to a directory in DOS.

Format: The physical specification for a page or a document.

Font/fount: A complete set of all sorts of the same typeface and point size.

Galley: Proofs pulled from a galley of type.

GEM: Graphics environment manager. A set of programs supplied by Digital Research.

H&J: Hyphenation and justification.

Half-tone: An illustration created by dots of varying size, resulting in the appearance of continuous tone.

Hard copy: Copy written, typed or printed as distinct from stored in electronic form.

House style: The typographic and linguistic rules of a publishing house.

Icon: A little picture on the screen, at which you can point to select the object that it represents.

IEEE: Institute of Electrical and Electronics Engineers. An American body that has proposed various standards, such as those for UNIX.

Justification: The spacing of words to a predetermined measure, giving 'straight' left and right margins.

Kern: Part of a typographic character projecting beyond the body.

Laser: A concentrated light beam with narrow width used in creating images, engraving, etc. 'Laser' is an acronym for 'light amplification by stimulated emission of radiation'.

Laser printer: A type of printer that uses similar technology to a photocopier.

Layout: Sketch of a page or spread of a book or other publication showing the plan to work to.

Leading: The spacing between lines of type (strips of lead in metal composition).

Lineale: A typeface without serifs, otherwise known as sans-serif.

Linotron: The high-speed cathode ray tube phototypesetting machines manufactured by Linotype.

Long run: A high printing number for a job.

Manuscript: Typed or handwritten copy for setting.

Matrix printer: A printer which produces its image in the form of a matrix of small dots. The term usually refers to an impact matrix printer, in which the dots are formed by pins striking a ribbon.

Mechanical: A camera-ready paste-up.

Memory: See *RAM* and *ROM.*

Montage: Several images assembled into one piece of artwork.

Mouse: A device with one or more buttons that is moved about on a flat surface to make a pointer or cursor move on the display screen.

MS-DOS: An operating system produced by Microsoft.

Multi-tasking: Able to process more than one program concurrently for the same user.

Multi-user: Able to accommodate more than one user of the system at a time.

Neckline: White space under a headline.

OCR: Optical character recognition. The interpretation of typewritten characters by a machine that scans the text and stores it in memory, often for subsequent typesetting.

Offset: Printing which uses an intermediate medium to transfer the image on to paper.

Page make-up: The assembly of the elements in a page into their final design.

Paste-up: A dummy comprising all the elements pasted into position.

Pixel: A 'picture element'; the smallest addressable element of a graphical display.

Phototypesetting: Setting type on to photographic paper or film.

Proofs: A trial printed sheet or copy, made before the production run for the purpose of checking.

Qwerty: Standard keyboard layout.

RAM: Random access memory. The main memory of a computer. It loses its data when the current is turned off.

ROM: Read-only memory.

RS232:   A standard for serial interface, used between computers and modems and for other purposes.

Sans serif: A typeface with no serifs.

Sector: A block of data on a disk.

Serial: A connection in which bits are sent one after another down a single wire.

Serif: The short cross line on the ends of ascenders, descenders and strokes of letters in certain typefaces.

Shift-click: To hold down the shift key while clicking with the mouse button, in order to select several items as a group.

Spooling: Printing a number of documents from a print queue, rather than directly from an application program.

Square serif: A typeface with serifs heavier than the strokes.

Text: The body typeset in a book or document.

Typeface: A specifically designed style of type, e.g. Times.

UNIX: A multi-user operating system invented by AT&T.

Vignette: A half-tone with the background fading out.

Widow: A short last line of a paragraph at the top of a page; considered undesirable.

WIMPs: Computer environment that contains windows, icons, mouse and pull-down menu.

Winchester: The type of fixed disk used in most personal computers.

Windows: A rectangular area on the display screen used by specific files or programs.

WYSIWYG: 'What you see is what you get.' An acronym used to describe a visual display that shows an exact replica of its output.

Index